The Journey of the Anointed One

Breakthrough to Spiritual Encounter

by

THEODORE J. NOTTINGHAM

Third Edition
2013

Third Edition

ISBN 9780983769712

Cover Art: Rebecca Nottingham

Icon by Andrei Rublev

Clipart Courtesy FCIT

Printed in the United States of America.

TABLE OF CONTENTS

PART II FRUITS OF THE JOURNEY

Preface

In the beginning was the word and the word was with God and the word was God. He was in the beginning with God. All things came into being through him and without him not one thing came into being. What has come into being in him was life and the life was the light of all people. The light shines in the darkness and the darkness did not overcome it. - John 1:1

These are some of the most marvelous words ever written by human beings inspired by Spirit. They're multi-dimensional and powerful, and it is my hope they will touch your soul even before you fully grasp what they may mean. Interestingly enough, this prologue of John begins with words that are strikingly similar to the first words of Genesis: *In the beginning God created...*

There is a connection – a connection between the creation of all things and the re-creation of the human spirit awakened to the reality of God. It's that cosmic of an event. Consider the famous Eagle Nebula captured by the Hubble Telescope and known as the Pillars of Creation, an awesome nursery for stars in deep space. Those columns are nine-and-a-half light years high! One light year is six trillion miles. It is inconceivable, yet there it is. This Nebula is 7,000 times six trillion miles away from us.

We cannot fathom that with our minds, but it is in this context and upon such a canvas that the Christ comes to us. It is out of the Uncreated One, the unimaginable, that we have a link, an intimate, life-altering human connection to that which is beyond all comprehension. How tragic it is that we have domesticated it and reduced it to a weekly habit and empty tradition, not to mention that we have blasphemed and rejected it as well. From the very beginning we are told that "*he came to his own and his own did not receive him.*"

This incredible event, which so changed human history, also changes our personal history, but it has been tragically misunderstood. Yet, we are constantly offered this opportunity to truly enter into connection with this gift, this reaching out from the heart of life itself to each of us. Let's go beyond surface dogma and into the depths. Let's enter into relationship with that which no one has seen and no one understands, except by this living connection through the journey of the Anointed One in this world.

Let me assure you that this is not exclusive to a particular religion, it does not require rejecting other spiritual intuitions from humanity. All the great teachings and sages of humanity, even the human heart itself, yearn for this connection, yearn for the Source, for home, for encounter with our true identity.

Here, in these timeless teachings from the Gospel of John, is the apex, the ultimate expression of that link with the Source. This is not merely a testimonial to a wise man, a good man, but to the *Logos* as it is said in Greek, to the mind of God, the principle of order of the universe manifested in fragile human flesh, so that we, even in our brief temporal existence, can have access to connection with God, the Uncreated.

To those who believe in him, who believe in his name he gave power to become children of God – "Who believe in his name" is a code word, not a mental agreement. To "believe in his name" is much more powerful than to sign on to a belief system or an intellectual concept.

In ancient Hebrew, the "word" had manifesting power in the world. In the story of Isaac's mistaken blessing of Jacob, Esau asks him to take the blessing back, but he cannot because he has given it out and its impact has taken place. This is an expression of the power of the word as the Hebrews understood it. We pay so little attention to what comes out of our mouths, yet that communication is an expression of who we are, and it affects the world around us.

"In the beginning was the Word..."

We like beginnings. We like to have a second chance, another opportunity *to get it right this time,* or at least to get on the right path and not go round and round in the same rut. But for change to take place, we must realize that "to believe in his name" means to cooperate, to participate with what is offered and to integrate that gift, that power, that spirit into our lives. This spiritual desire enables us to go deeper, to find new meaning, to become that vaster person, that child of God we truly are...the one who is our true identity.

We must make a goal of addressing those flaws and infirmities in ourselves that we know need work. This requires honesty with oneself, which is always painful. Yet, these are the very things that keep us locked in the basement of ourselves. It is not acceptable to be a mean-spirited human being and to claim to "believe in His name." That's just a lot of talk...it's the words without the music.

From the beginning of human wisdom, self-knowledge has been critical if one is to progress. Work on it. Deal with it, and be open to it. Observe who you are and what comes out of you. It's called spiritual warfare, and it's a noble act. It will bring you to a new place spiritually, experientially, mentally, emotionally and psychologically. Resolution, prayer, commitment to God, and facing the fact that you'll experience opposition – are what comprise the spiritual journey made available to us by the Anointed One.

We are fragmented beings. We need to pull together all those pieces of ourselves that want to make such efforts, and leave the rest behind. That's why it is called the *narrow way*. There is much you can't take with you on this journey, and you have to be ready for the opposition. You have to plan on it, and you have to know that it's the battle of David and Goliath within yourself.

The Lord brought me forth as the first of his works before his deed of old. I was appointed from eternity from the beginning before the world began. There has always been this knowledge that the wisdom, the *Sophia* of God, the expression of God, was accessible and was communicating to each of us. Regardless of whatever foolishness humanity has made of religion, misusing it from the beginning – from the Jerusalem Church that did not want to preach, to the Greeks, to the countless forms of misunderstandings and abuses that have claimed to know the Truth – it is our turn now. Each of us is called to understand how personal it is, how up close it is, how in the middle of your ordinary afternoon is the decision, is the resolution to make this moment of your life shine with spirit. Let spirit in, let it break the bonds of the old worldly habits, dare to risk for the unknown, for that deeper self, for that nearness of God that is the gift from the Holy One to each of us.

PART I

THE JOURNEY

1

The Preparation

The beginning of the good news of Jesus Christ, the Son of God.

As it is written by the prophet Isaiah,
"See, I am sending my messenger ahead of you,
who will prepare your way;
the voice of one crying out in the wilderness:
'Prepare the way of the Lord,
make his paths straight.' "

John the baptizer appeared in the wilderness, proclaiming a baptism of repentance for the forgiveness of sins. And people from the whole Judean countryside and all the people of Jerusalem were going out to him, and were baptized by him in the river Jordan, confessing their sins. Now John was clothed with camel's hair, with a leather belt around his waist, and he ate locusts and wild honey. He proclaimed, "The one who is more powerful than I is coming after me; I am not worthy to stoop down and untie the thong of his sandals. I have baptized you with water; but he will baptize you with the Holy Spirit." - Mark 1: 1-8

I imagine these words are familiar to most of us. What we have here is more than a story, of course. Let me put it in its historical context. Four hundred years have gone by since a prophet has spoken to the people of Israel – it's a time of barrenness, abandonment and decay. The people have become so faithless that there seems to be no sign of God anywhere among them. Four hundred years…that is almost twice the length of the history of the United States. It has been a long, barren period, even though Isaiah and

Moses had prophesied that someday, as the Holy One had communicated to them these words: *"I will send to you…"* The last of the prophets, Malachi, in the last book of the Old Testament, also gives out that same vision: *"I will send my messenger."*

Then, out of the blue, in the midst of the wilderness appears this odd person, this outsider, this radical holy man preaching a baptism of repentance. What he taught was not a tradition of the Jews. This was a break with tradition. This was a new thing appearing in the world, and a new thing that can enter into our personal lives. This is not a history lesson or a lesson in religion. This is wisdom for us right now. What this long awaited prophet brought to humanity was an opportunity to experience *Emmanuel,* God among us, in a new way.

The reference to "the wilderness" is not just a geographical location. The wilderness is the place where everyone ends up, where we all must go to find ourselves. Who has not walked through barrenness, pain, loneliness and hopelessness? These ancient scriptures point out that it is precisely in that environment – where nothing is helping us, where we feel that we are lost forever – that a preparation begins for a new relationship with Spirit!

Out of that internal wilderness there always seems to be one voice crying out to us. It is never the popular opinion. It is never politically correct. It always comes as a shocker and shakes us up, just as John the Baptist was shaking people up. To the Hebrew people, baptism, or ritual washing, was a form of purification. No one was immersed among the Chosen People. The Essene sect, living in the Qumran Community nearby, had ritual washing every morning as part of their holistic sense of purification. They washed their hearts as they washed their hands.

Then John comes along and asks his people to take on that immersion baptism which only the gentiles underwent to become members of their religion. In other words, he was telling them (and us) that we have to start all over again. We must become awakened children of the Uncreated One, which requires a new beginning as part of the preparation to experience the Christ event.

In modern terms it would sound like this: *Just because you've come to church all this time is not good enough. There has to be a spiritual transformation or the appearance of the Anointed One is missed, taken for granted, stored away in a corner of your life instead of being the center of a new beginning.* What is commonly called "repentance" is a poor translation of *Metanoia* which means metamorphosis, change of mind, change of attitudes. This is what John was preaching.

Imagine if we understood that this "turning around" was about becoming people of light, bright natured, happy people – that would be Good News indeed. In fact, that was the preparation announced by John: to be cleansed inwardly and to finally reach our true potential, our purpose in this world. But repentance has meant guilt, feeling bad, and self-hatred. If you have reason to feel bad about something, don't let it last too long because this is not the purpose of this teaching. The Good News is to remove the guilt and then move on to a new way of living.

Euangelion is the Greek word for "gospel" or "good news." It was a term used for the emperor's victory and it was passed on for the Anointed One in reference to God's victory in humanity...in your life. This is about God's victory in your life over against all that is not God. You know what that is, don't you? What do you think it means that there was no room at the inn? It's the inn within our heart. There is no room for Spirit in our heart because we have not cleansed it. You cannot remain the same and experience God in your life. You cannot spend all week full of toxic behavior, then sing a few songs and hope everything will be fine.

Holy Spirit needs a pure heart in which to dwell and so John was calling all humanity, regardless of "pedigree," to start fresh. Recognize your need and begin. This is not an old religion; this is an eternal cosmic teaching where Christ is born in your heart every time you open it up. Angelus Silesius says that it doesn't matter if Christ was born a thousand times in Bethlehem, if he's not born in your heart. The journey of Christ through this world, from its very beginning, is about our own encounter with Spirit.

So this strange prophet in the desert appeared on the human scene and broke all the rules, proclaiming that the Kingdom, or the Presence of God, is not in the future, but is "at hand." You will recall that Jesus said, *of all the seekers in the world, John was the greatest and yet he is the least in the Kingdom.* The Anointed One who came to baptize with the Holy Spirit brings humanity to a new level that surpasses the spirituality of the tradition of the prophets.

That's why we are told that John wore camel's hair and lived out the harsh disciplines of the old religion. Jesus says: "Up until now the Kingdom of Heaven is taken by force, by violent men..." In other words, until the advent of the Anointed One, something was lacking in the search for God. It was a kind of seeking of Truth without goodness, including goodness toward oneself.

So he was taking the old ways and putting them aside for something totally new. Jesus does that all the time – He brings something totally new into your life that enables you to taste, to see, and to be transformed.

2

Wilderness

Then Jesus was led up by the Spirit into the wilderness to be tempted by the devil. And he fasted forty days and forty nights, and afterward he was hungry. And the tempter came and said to him, "If you are the Son of God, command these stones to become loaves of bread." But he answered, "It is written, 'Man shall not live by bread alone, but by every word that proceeds from the mouth of God.' " Then the devil took him to the holy city, and set him on the pinnacle of the temple, and said to him, "If you are the Son of God, throw yourself down; for it is written, 'He will give his angels charge of you,' and 'On their hands they will bear you up, lest you strike your foot against a stone.' " Jesus said to him, "Again it is written, 'You shall not tempt the Lord your God.' " Again, the devil took him to a very high mountain, and showed him all the kingdoms of the world and the glory of them; and he said to him, "All these I will give you, if you will fall down and worship me." Then Jesus said to him, "Begone, Satan! for it is written, 'You shall worship the Lord your God and him only shall you serve.' " Then the devil left him, and behold, angels came and ministered to him. - Matthew 4:1-11

What we have before us is not a story, not a narrative, not a biographical note. It is a spiritual teaching. It is encapsulated in images and words and sent down through time to you right now. This is for you. This is not about somebody else. Jesus is the first fruits of many, meaning that he walks that path to show *us* how to walk that path.

Jesus goes into our dark places in order to bring us out of them. For these scriptures to mean something, they have to bring hope to someone who needs strength and wisdom, and that someone is every one of us. Jesus was led into the wilderness. The wilderness is not a place. It is not about the desert in Judea. The wilderness is a state of mind, a state of our emotions. It is that place that every one of us knows – that place of pain, of loneliness, and hopelessness. It is the place of feeling abandoned by God. Don't you know that place? All of us have found ourselves in it, the place where there seems to be no help. But then the help comes in your wilderness, in your private, unspoken wilderness.

The teaching tells us that Jesus is led by the Spirit into the wilderness. Sometimes we have to walk through those empty places to find our way to a higher understanding. It's not that God wants us to suffer. God forbid we should follow that primitive thinking. But even in the darkest places, we can learn, grow, and come out into the light. That's the beauty of this revelation, that at the very heart of life, in the mundane, in the ridiculous, in the horrible, we can learn, grow, and awaken to the power of God right in the midst of our life.

So bring to mind that place for you that you can call "wilderness," which no one knows about but you. You're the only one there. The term "temptation" is a code word, and does not refer to what we might understand as temptation. This is not about being tempted by an ice cream sundae, by lust, or by anything else. This is the *fundamental spiritual temptation.* Do I put my way first or God's way? This is the crossroads for every human being – the heart of the matter, the spiritual battle in which the Holy One engages so that we can know how to come through victoriously.

We can read all sorts of things and have all kinds of experiences, but only the *Man of sorrows acquainted with grief* can take us through those dark places in the wilderness to be tempted by "the devil." It is easy to make this universe a duality and think of some objective creature, to put a tail on it with wings, but that's not what this is about.

This is much more personal. It is up close and personal, because it is inside of us – that temptation to not go God's way, but to have our own way; the temptation to not care about spiritual matters in a world that rejects them; the temptation to live the old way, to do anything without accountability – that is the devil within. The devil comes from the word *Diabolos* which means *the slanderer*, or that which slanders the things of God. What are the things of God? Not high holy things, but goodness, compassion, forgiveness, righteousness and kindness. Don't you see how mean-spiritedness poisons the well? It ruins the possibilities; it breaks us away from our true destiny.

So we don't need some epic spiritual image or an idea that rises out of Milton's "Paradise Lost." It's in the little things; it's in the everyday things where you are tempted to make the choice to care only about yourself and not about someone else's feelings or needs; to disregard what God would have you do. That's demonic. That's the ungodly, and it is easy to make it metaphysical, because then you can just believe it or not. It doesn't really fit into our world view. But when it's right there at the center of your heart, your mind and your psychology, there is no escaping that we *have to make a choice.*

Each one of us can begin to get a taste of that within us which is unholy and ungodly. Your job as a Christian is to get it "behind you" and say: *"I'm going another way,"* so then that which would have you disregard the things of God, in essence, cries out to the holy one: *Make bread of these stones,* because he is famished. All of us are famished. We are famished for understanding; famished for wisdom; famished for God's Presence.

The Greek word used here is *epiousios*, which means *bread from above,* or super substantial bread, or *spiritual wisdom* – asking for enlightenment from God, for inspiration and guidance. A life without meaning is the worst possible life. We must discover the true meaning of our lives in order to possess a true life. Yet, we are tempted as Jesus was, to invent our own meaning. The whole world around us is a distraction for this process – for the temptation to make our own meaning for the purpose of our existence. That's why Jesus says: *I am fed by the word of God. I am fed by truth. I am fed by the deeper things.*

We are spirit encased in matter, and we must remember who we are, *whose* we are, and why we're here, in order to come out of the wilderness. Without a compass, without any sense of who we truly are, we are lost. We have no real meaning. We just respond to the horrors of life, the accidents, the illnesses and the mistakes, and life is nothing more than an endless tragedy.

The Anointed One is called the Savior because he reveals to us how to live a life that is full, joyful, hopeful and meaningful. That is salvation, not some strange theological idea, but a palpable reality, where every day is filled to the brim with abundant life because you've got your priorities straight. You have realigned your perspective. You're at peace because *God is,* and all things work for good for those who love of God.

Next in the metaphorical temptations of Christ, is the invitation for him to jump off the highest temple in Jerusalem, be caught by angels and carried away. What does that mean? How is that related to your life? It's about self-glory and self-importance. Can you imagine how much easier it would have been for Jesus of Nazareth to put on a big show to amaze the world? Kings from the farthest corners of earth would have come to bow down to him. But they weren't going to bow down to the man of sorrows who went to the cross.

This is the ego's effort to stay alive, to take the way out, to avoid being crucified on the way to a higher life. So that temptation is very real for us. We witness it in our desire to be recognized, our insistence on having the last word, or our need to be loved by everyone.

The next temptation that comes from the unholy tells us that all the riches of this world belong to him. From this we learn that although possessions in themselves are not bad, when they have become our meaning, when materialism is our purpose in life, then it has turned demonic; it belongs to that which is ungodly. So in this world full of sharks, of *taking care of number one*, of trying to get as many toys as possible, we are given that universal Truth that all you'll end up with is wilderness, emptiness.

Again, in the world around us, we see that people are attempting to create their own ideas of what's important. Then they crash and burn. They end up nowhere. But this beautiful secret teaching is for those who truly love God, who know that Christ comes to give us new life. And if we apply it specifically to the details of our life, we will be led out of the wilderness. We will come out of that darkness and into the light. We will no longer be fooled or lied to by that within us which will not turn to God. So you must find that thing within you and confront it, whatever it is, that part of you which will not turn to God. Find that willfulness, find that selfishness, that foolishness or stubbornness, and know that it is *Diabolos*. It is what will keep you from God. It is what will keep you lost in the wilderness of unhappiness.

Next we are told that after Christ had endured these temptations, after he had shown us the way, that angels came and ministered to him. Herein is another teaching, and it is this: If you apply these teachings, if you give the best you have, you will be ministered to by that which is higher and greater than yourself. You will be lifted up in your hour of need. You will be given guidance and joy and peace that is beyond your understanding.

And finally, in another gospel, we are told that the devil left to come back at an opportune time. From this teaching we learn that we must always remain on guard for that which would keep us from walking the path of the Anointed One in this world.

3

The Invitation

In ancient times, finding a teacher of spiritual truth was the pearl of great price. Once you found such a person you stayed with them, you lived with them, you learned from them. The chosen ones – the chosen people as a nation – were hungry for knowing the ways of pleasing God and connecting with the living Spirit. So the rabbi was of great significance. We have here in the Gospel of John, written in Greek for Greek readers, the definition of *rabbi.* The term means "teacher." In Hebrew, it means "my great one."

Seekers and disciples loved their spiritual teachers. They received life giving food from them. So to leave their teacher was unheard of, yet we find John the Baptist doing the unthinkable by telling his students: *Go with Him now, because something new has come into the world.* This was unprecedented, and an extraordinary turn of events that transcended all the wisdom and tradition of the Hebrews down through the ages. So these faithful followers of the prophet John left him, and as they came to Jesus, we have the very first words of the Master as presented in the Gospel of John.

His very first words are: *What are you seeking?* You may be sure that he is not talking to those disciples only. He is asking that question of you and me. This is the eternal spirit saying to you – *What are you seeking as the deepest meaning of your existence? What is the most important thing to you in life? What is that yearning within you that you've tried to suppress by doing everything else but seeking after it?*

When you hunger for God, when you need connection with Spirit, you begin to seek. A wonderful philosopher says: "It is only when you realize that life is leading you nowhere that it begins to have meaning." It is only when you realize that all the material things of life are not satisfying, that a profound personal yearning generates within you a spiritual journey.

To become a disciple of Jesus you have to want something more than what the world provides. You have to know that nothing can satisfy this deep yearning, yet most of us spend a lifetime trying to quiet that yearning – through alcohol, pills, distractions or material things. We will do almost anything not to be face to face with the deepest yearning of our soul where that cosmic question resonates – *What are you seeking? What is most important to you?*

So the disciples responded by asking: *"Where are you staying?"* This is where it is critical to not read the Bible literally, or on the surface. For thousands of years, the teachers of Christianity have referred to multiple dimensions of meaning, that in fact you must read in a state of prayer so that inspiration from Spirit can awaken you to the depths of Holy Scripture. That is why it is called "holy," and it is a tragic mistake to reduce it to the surface level.

Do you think the disciples wanted to know in which motel Jesus was staying on the outskirts of Nazareth? The clue that this is spiritual is that the word for "staying" is found in very important places in the Gospel of John. *"Abide [stay] in me and I in you." - John 15:4*

They were asking this holy man: *What is the rock that you stand on? What is it that gives you courage? What is it that gives you peace in the midst of trouble? What is the center of your being?* And

He responds, *"Come and see!"* That word "see" does not merely mean "look at it" – it means *come and experience* – find out for yourself. We have to find out organically what he comes to reveal. This is not a belief system or an opinion. It is conscious awareness of the truth that he reveals, and that is what makes a disciple of Christ. Once such a truth is revealed to a person's heart, the first thing this person wants to do is to share what he or she has found! The first thing Andrew does is to find his brother Simon and exclaim *"We have found the Messiah!"* and later we find Philip running to Nathaniel, then John running to James.

Within a hundred years of this moment, Christianity is all over the world. How? Why? Not good marketing, not bells and whistles and gimmicks. One at a time, one person going to another person. If each of you here found the transformational peace, the strength of connection with spirit that you just had to share with another friend, you would be growing Christianity. That is the secret, and it began at the very beginning.

The secret to be shared is *change, transformation.* We find Jesus saying to Peter – you will no longer be called Simon, you'll now be called Peter. Semitic Hebrew understanding of names held that a name reveals the inner nature of a thing. This is why Moses wanted to know the name of God. Unfortunately, he was given even more mystery with the revelation of the Name: *"I Am the One who Is."* That name suggests a "quantum" identity. So when Jesus changed Simon's name, he was changing his nature, leading him toward becoming a new person, a wholly new creation. Such a transformation does not happen right away. One of the worst mistakes of bad theology is to profess that we are born again in an instant, dunked in the water and you're done. No, it is a transformational process. It is about making a choice in every moment between going the old way, the automatic way, the knee jerk reaction way, or going the Christ Way. When you get in the car with your spouse and something is said that offends you, there is your opportunity – which way are you going to go? Are you going to be Simon or will you be Peter? You know you can ruin a whole day with one unkind reaction.

As we continue in the Gospel of John, we see where Jesus decides to go to Galilee. We are given the words: "*Finding Philip…*" Consider these two words. He has just said *"What are you seeking?"* and now he is "finding Philip." What does that mean? Philip is not looking for Jesus, it is Jesus who finds him. This is a reversal...the other side of the coin. It tells us that God has to grab some of us by the scruff of the neck and lift us up out of our selfishness, our foolishness and our ignorance. That is part of the wonder of God. *God is looking for us more than we are looking for God.* Sometimes we are going in the other direction, and there comes a knock on the door of our heart. If we decide not to answer it, the door might be kicked in. God comes into your life and says: *"Where have you been?"*

Upon finding Philip, Jesus says *"Follow me."* Now *follow me* doesn't really give the full import of these extraordinary words. We figure it is a passive act, sort of like the march of the penguins, just following along in line. But the Greek word means *walk alongside me on the journey.* It even implies *"imitate me."*

In French, the verb for follow is *suivre.* So Jesus says: "*Suis moi.*" However, you may know that you can say *Je suis* which means *I am.* So, "*Suis moi*" in French also means

"Become me!" Following Jesus is not a passive, brainless thing, but rather a *transformation* into a Christ-like pattern of being. That is what the call to "follow me" really means.

Philip then runs to Nathaniel and the teaching becomes very interesting at this point. Nathaniel is you and me. Nathaniel is in Cana, four miles from Nazareth. He is one of those rational disciples and he says: *Well, Nazareth is just a dumpy little village with a Roman Garrison in it*, or as it is stated in Scripture: *"Can anything good come out of Nazareth?"*

We are all guilty of not seeing the world as it really is, as the quantum physicists or the poets see it. William Blake, for instance, saw infinity in a grain of sand. We are all moving so quickly that we are missing the wonder of being alive. In other words, we are missing the Presence of God.

So here is Nathaniel the cynic who dares to wonder in Jesus' presence – *"Can anything good come out of Nazareth?"* Philip says *"Come and see, come and find out for yourself."* Instead of being offended, Jesus responds: *"Here is a true Israelite in whom there is no guile, in whom there is nothing false."* In other words, he sees Nathaniel for who he really is in spite of Nathaniel's cynicism.

Nathaniel says something offensive, demeaning, ignorant and petty, and Jesus reacts with an unexpected response – *"Look at that beautiful soul."* Jesus does not see who you are in all your unpleasantness and prejudices, he sees what you can be, what you ought to be, what you have been, what you want to be. If you need self-esteem, begin to realize that God sees you as the best that you can become. So you can put aside all the negatives, all the sin, all the limitations, all the things your spouse says about you, and realize that God sees your true potential.

Nathaniel is astonished and cries out: *"How do you know me?"* Imagine that scene. That is our question – *God, how do you know me?* Ask yourself that primal question: *How do you know me?* God knows you better than you know yourself, and loves you anyway. When Nathaniel asks him *"how do you know me,"* Jesus says: *"I saw you while you were under the fig tree."* The fig tree wasn't just a bush in a corner. He didn't say to Nathaniel, *I saw you over there next to the bushes.* The fig tree was the sweetest fruit of the desert. The rabbis taught in the shade of the fig tree. It was also a sacred place of prayer and meditation; a place of yearning for Messiah. So it symbolized something very significant. In the Book of Micah, we read: *"Every man will sit under his own vine, under his own fig tree and no one will make them afraid."* Zachariah writes that *"on that day each of you will invite his neighbor to sit under his vine and fig tree."* In other words, there is deeper meaning to the fig tree. Jesus saw in the spirit Nathaniel under that symbolic tree. Perhaps Nathaniel was praying there. Jesus saw his heart and the sincerity of his worship. Can you imagine the feeling of knowing that God sees you when you pray, even if there seems to be no answer? That, in itself, ought to be a source of great comfort and hope.

So Jesus sees clairvoyantly that in that moment this young man, in spite of his cynicism, was seeking the Holy. Then Nathaniel cries out: *"You are the son of God, the king of Israel!"* and Jesus tells him and each of us that we will see much greater things than this. He is telling us that we all have the possibility of experiencing the mystery and wonder of Spirit in this time and place through being a follower, a disciple, an imitator of Christ.

The way to witness and see spirit is simply: Come and see. Come and experience. Come and taste. That is a message for every person. Life can change radically, it can be known as sacred. You can find peace in your heart even when nothing is going well. This is what Jesus is saying – Come find out what you are really meant to know and experience in this life.

4

The Core Teachings

We have before us in Matthew chapter 5, the very core of Jesus' teaching and purpose for being among us. This is the essence of what he taught, the very heart of everything he said. This is the nucleus, the transforming axis of Jesus' revelation of divine wisdom, so what follows are holy words which I hope you can receive in a new way – a way that reaches deep inside of you, inside of your issues, inside of your greatest desires.

Even before we touch on those extraordinary words of blessedness, we find a great teaching. At the very beginning of the chapter we are told that he *went up the mountain.* The Hebrews were a great mystical people for whom everything was connected to God and to the sacred mystery of life. So to go up the mountain, as Moses did on Mount Sinai, is to prepare for the reception of a cosmic revelation. When we hear that Jesus goes up the mountain, it is time to listen carefully because what is going to come next is from the heart of the living God.

We are given another ordinary statement preceding this teaching: *He sat down.* In synagogues everywhere, before commenting on the Scriptures, the rabbi would sit in the seat of Moses as it was called. So the act of sitting down is the preparation for bringing authoritative teaching to the people. He sat to give his inspired teachings, as the rabbis do in the synagogues. In the Gospel of Luke, there is a verse that says: *He raised his head and looked at his disciples.* Yet they were surrounded on all sides by a great crowd. So he is not talking to the crowd, he is talking to you, the disciple; to you, the one who is hungry for God.

Blessed are the poor in spirit.

We cannot even begin to understand these words if we take them literally, on the surface, or thoughtlessly. Clearly, we are told right off the bat that when he talks about "the poor in spirit," he does not mean the financially poor! He is referring to a spiritual condition. What does it mean to be so poor in spirit that you will be blessed? And what does this word "blessed" mean? The Greek word *makarios*, translated as *blessed*, means that you will be blissfully, ecstatically happy. It infers that if you were in that spiritual state referred to as *poor in spirit*, you would get out of your doldrums and experience the joy of being alive in every moment of your existence!

In Luke, we find four "woes" following these beatitudes in reference to those who are "rich," and the reason for this curse is, in the Master's words, *"for you have already received your comfort."* Again, this is not about bank accounts, this is not class warfare. The "rich in spirit" are those who are filled with their pride, vanity, and all of their issues. They are filled with themselves and with all that we human beings are subject to that is unlovely and ungodly. This is the condition referred to in Psalm 10: *"The wicked are too proud to seek God. God is in none of their thoughts."*

Imagine being so filled with your own self-absorption that there is no room for God – that is what it means to be "rich." So to be *poor in spirit* is to live in that *humility that knows it is fully dependent on God.* It means that you must empty yourself of all your self-interest that is so easily offended, that is always worried about what other people think of you, and that is constantly seeking attention. This is the source of so much of our misery. When we let it all go, Jesus says that we will indeed be blissful in that new humility and simplicity of spirit, dependent on God, focused on God, and finally free of so much unnecessary suffering due to obsession with ourselves.

Blessed are they that mourn,
for they shall be comforted.

Isn't this a strange paradox? This is the good news. This is about salvation, holiness, healing, happiness. We find in this great teaching, Jesus himself saying, *"these things I have spoken to you that my joy may be in you and that your joy may be complete."* Yet here he says seemingly that it is a blessed thing to mourn. We've got to do some extra listening here.

Most of us have mourned over the many loses of life, the disappointments and the sorrows. But Jesus is speaking to us of a *different kind* of mourning. What kind of mourning would it be that would bring blessedness to our lives? Let me point to the Apostle Paul and his wonderful words: *"When I want to do good, evil is right there with me."*

He speaks for all of us when he states: *"For I delight in the law of God in my inmost self, but I see in my members another law at war with the law of my mind, making me captive to the law of sin that dwells in my members."* We are mourning for the fact that we are so distant from God and in the painful knowledge that it is so hard to get past our personalities, our wounds, our weaknesses, our Achilles heels, to please God. In Second Corinthians Chapter 7, we read: *"For godly grief produces a repentance that leads to salvation."* In Revelations we are told that *"He will wipe away every tear from their eyes."*

God wants you to be happy. He wants you to be blessed – that is part of the salvific revelation that is given to us by our Lord. So to mourn is to be one of those who yearns for that spiritual connection, who knows that without it, life is barren and meaningless, and who mourns the fact that God is not at the center of their lives, that they still have not found that pathway that links us to spirit. The pathway is found right here in these beatitudes.

Blessed are the meek for they shall inherit the earth.

How we have misunderstood that one! Just because meek rhymes with "weak" does not mean that this is the meaning of that word. The Greek word for meek is *praus*, which means: *Great power under control.* Think of the taming of a wild animal in order to domesticate it, to align its great power under the control of the master.

In the Book of Numbers, we find that Moses was described as "very meek above all men." Remember Moses? Moses who walked up to Ramses, the greatest pharaoh of Egypt and the most powerful tyrant in the world at the time, and said: *"Let my people go!"* There is nothing weak about that. Or how about Jesus saying: *"Take my yoke upon you for I am meek and lowly in heart,"* and he is the one who, without blinking, walks to the cross, to the most horrific form of death imagined in the dark side of man's mind, and faces those nine inch nails for all of us to receive this teaching.

So next time you hear that word "meek" don't associate it with weak and timid. It is referring to God-controlled powers, to your powers given over to God's purposes. The opposite of that word *praus* in Greek, is "anger." In our culture we think anger is strong, don't we? In the movies, our heroes get angry all the time and that's when we think they are powerful. But the divine wisdom that Christ bled and died for tells us that *anger is weakness,* instability, the fragmentation of who we are meant to be. To be meek is to not allow yourself to fall into the insanity of anger. How many of us have gotten terribly angry and then in one minute, ten minutes, or half an hour, wish we had another chance to do it over differently? Anger is not a good thing if you're seeking God.

Blessed are they that hunger and thirst after righteousness.

We hear in the Psalms *"my soul thirsts for you, my body longs for you in a dry and weary land where there is no water..."* And again, *"For he satisfies the thirsty and fills the hungry with good things."* This is not a reference to food for the body, but rather food for the soul. Jesus says: "*I am the bread of life. He who comes to me will not be hungry.*" Who wants to come into the heart of God and be useful to God? Who hungers for that? Blessed are you if you hunger for that!

Our world today tries very hard to push that out of existence, to make it pointless, to reduce reality to paying taxes. Stay strong in your hunger for the meaning of life, for the reality of God. Blessed are you says our Lord. He also says: *"My food is to do the will of Him who sent me and to finish His work."* It is the same for us.

Blessed are the merciful for they shall obtain mercy.

Jesus says "*Be merciful as my father is merciful.*" How are we to be merciful? What is mercy? Mercy is not justice. Mercy is given to someone when they don't deserve it. Mercy is the ability to forgive. How do we learn to do that? How do we manifest mercy in that godly way? Only when we value and know *how much mercy God has shown to us.* It is only when we begin to realize the depth of our sinful nature, that we begin to understand the depth of his mercy and forgiveness. Most of us are not criminals; we haven't done anything monstrous in life. But even in the little things, we all know we need forgiveness. We need forgiveness for not loving at the right time, not loving enough, or for not being available to someone when they needed us. God forgives us again and again, and when we know that in our heart of hearts, then we understand it is time for us to do the same for others.

Blessed are the pure in heart, for they shall see God.

The word "pure" comes from *katharos* in Greek, from which we get the word catharsis, which in turn means – purging, cleansing like the silver that has to be refined. How is this done? The refining process requires that all the dirt from the bottom be brought to the surface, making it one unmixed substance. In other words, it is the process of creating a heart that has no wickedness in it, where those other substances are removed. The refiner knows that he has finished his task when he looks into the molten silver and sees his reflection. Consider the implications of that metaphor: When God can see God's reflection in your heart, your heart has been cleansed. When goodness, compassion, mercy, forgiveness and love are in your heart, your heart is purified. Not only can God see God's reflection, you can "see" God. You can understand in a new way. You can find God in others. It is authentic transformation.

Blessed are the peacemakers.

The old translation states: "for they shall be called sons of God." Of course it is for men and women alike, but understand its meaning: Jesus says "they shall be called sons of God." Isn't that the very title of Jesus – Son of God? When we become peacemakers, we will be called the very thing Jesus is called! But you can't give what you don't have. To be a peacemaker, you must first make peace with yourself before you can make peace with others. You must make peace with God and God's will in your life. When you discover this – when you make peace with your own destiny, you will enter into the peace and rest of God, and only then can you become a transmitter of peace to others.

If five people in our congregation were completely centered on peacemaking, they would radiate peace out to everyone else, and that would change the congregation, the community, and the world. But if we allow ourselves to be the angry one, the envious one, the gossiping one, we are not blessed. We have not entered this path that Christ has called us to travel upon today.

Blessed are those who are persecuted for righteousness' sake.

The Gospel of Luke states: *"Blessed are you when men hate you, when they exclude you and insult you and revile you in my name."* Someone once said that three things will happen to you when you really become a Christian:

You will lose all your fears, because in your poverty of spirit you will trust in God no matter what; you will be happy when you go outside and see the beauty of the world; and you will be happy even if someone offends you, because you know that God is present in your life.

The human world works in darkness and tends to gravitate toward the ungodly. Those who seek to be centered in God are going against the current, against the herd, and when that happens they will eat you alive. You know that everybody wants you to share in their nastiness, in their negativity, in their rage: *Come and join us so we can reinforce our reality. We don't want to know about another reality.*

So you have to stand firm, stand strong, like Luther said: *"Here I stand."* That is the moment you step onto the path, and not before. We must be mindful of the words from Jesus, in John 15: "*Remember the word that I spoke to you? A servant is not above his master. If they persecuted me they will persecute you.*"

So the next time you try to do good and it blows up in your face, don't get angry, and don't be surprised. Not only did Jesus foretell this for you, he *went* before you! You are in good company. Stay on the path and remember that all these blessed ways are not referring to different people. We are meant to go through all these stages. We are meant to be blessed if we mourn, blessed if we hunger, blessed if we are poor in spirit, and blessed if we are pure in heart. These are the varied ways in which each of us truly enters the path of Christ, the Way of life traced by the Savior.

5

Becoming Disciples

What does the word "disciple" mean? The Greek word means *student, learner or pupil.* One who goes to the Master when they become aware that they need to learn something new, when they know that they don't know. Down through history, there have always been seekers looking for the one with wisdom, one who knows a little more. These seekers make gigantic efforts to follow that star in their heart, that need to find meaning in life. Followers of Christ are students, and therefore we never stop learning. We never stop looking at that horizon where new discoveries await us – not only that external horizon, but the internal one, the undiscovered country within.

So we read in John 8 that "He then began to teach them." But this is Chapter 8. He has been teaching ever since he said *"Repent, for the Kingdom of Heaven is at hand,"* yet we are told that he "then began to teach them." In other words, it has now become teaching of a new depth, a new level. It is advanced teaching for those who really desire to walk the Way of Christ. These teachings take place shortly after Peter recognizes that Jesus is the Christ, the Anointed One. Then, Jesus opens the door to an entirely new and unexpected teaching when he reveals that he must be persecuted and rejected, tortured and killed.

The Messiah, whom everyone thought would ride in on a great war horse and save the day, bringing the justice of God that would make the earth a paradise, is now revealed as "a man of sorrows, acquainted with grief." The Christ is that truth and goodness and compassion that is going to be persecuted, that is, rejected through history, even right down to this very today.

Most shocking of all is that it's religious people, quite often, who do the persecuting! So he is giving them a double shock: all the good people, the Elders, the Pharisees, the ones that are highly respected, who know well the teachings of God, will lead the persecution. That was incomprehensible, and it should be incomprehensible to us today. Why would religious people persecute Truth and goodness? The answer is very simple – we are frail human beings.

All of us must be watchful, and keep an eye out so as not to fall off the edge of that narrow path. Any one of us is capable of slipping, of turning violent, of losing ourselves and forgetting God's call on our lives. It's the nature of being human. This is not about ancient history, it's about us here and now, because Christ is crucified every time truth and goodness are persecuted.

So now Peter, upon hearing Christ tell of his own persecution, says, like us: *No, absolutely not! This cannot happen!* We're all outraged by this injustice, and it is a natural reaction. It's the human reaction. Yet, here again, Jesus gives us another powerful teaching in those strange and familiar words he speaks to Peter, *"Get behind me Satan!"*

That word *Satan* is a Hebrew word meaning "the adversary." It means the adversary of God – that which is opposed to God's ways; that which is ungodly. In this case, Jesus is pointing out that to think in the normal human way is to be an adversary of God. To see a situation without God in it, to think that those are the dynamics of that reality and forget about God's Presence is satanic, is against reality, is to be an adversary of Truth.

So this is a calling to all of us to keep God in the picture, to trust his will and his ways, and that's not always easy to do, as our logical minds forget about it. It is totally paradoxical, and yet we are called to do precisely that – to keep the sacred in the picture over and above what our minds can understand. When we fail in this, we oppose God's purpose and will for our lives. How many times have we been in situations that seem so terribly hopeless, and yet, when all was said and done, somehow Spirit made something beautiful of it.

Next, we read that Jesus called everyone around him. He asks us to focus now, to bend an ear, to listen carefully to what he is going to say. He is going to tell us three things. He begins by saying: "*If anyone would come after me...*" We have to stop right there because that is a big "if." *If* you are one who really wants to commit themselves to the things of the Spirit – to that which the eye generally cannot see and which other people are not interested in – *if* you are that person...

There is a great deal of ourselves that is not interested. He is talking to that little part of us, that little piece of will power that wants to live for God, that knows in the heart of hearts that unconditional goodness is the purpose of life. The Anointed One is telling that part of our being what we must do: "*If anyone would follow me, they must deny themselves.*"

He is not saying that you must hate yourself. Let's get that clear, because throughout history those words have led people to become masochistic to the point of inhumanity toward themselves and others. Let me remind you that it is

Jesus who said: *"I came to bring you life – life in abundance; I came to make your joy complete;"* and *"Enter into the joy of your master."*

Welcome to the mysteries of spiritual paradoxes. We are to deny ourselves in order to find joy. That is quantum physics of the spirit. Don't take it as beating your body or denying yourself the basics of life. That is not what he is saying. He is saying – deny that part of you that does not want to go the way of loving-kindness.

Most of our behavior is reacting to people and circumstances, and when we come down off the ceiling an hour later or the next day, we either wish we hadn't done it or we have a big mess to clean up. Wouldn't it be wonderful before we hit that ceiling if something in us reminded us to deny that part of ourselves? And wouldn't it be wonderful if we listened? Save yourself and everybody else the trouble of cleaning up the misery. Deny that typical habit and reaction. How life would be different!

In order to live this we way, we must "take up our cross." In the first century, everyone knew what that meant. They had seen people going up the hill dragging a cross over their shoulder, surrounded by Roman soldiers. Everyone knew they weren't coming back. The road to Jerusalem was lined with hundreds of crosses. The Romans knew how to intimidate people. It was the worst kind of one way street, and Jesus uses this as a spiritual metaphor on how to enter the Christ way, God's way, the way of loving-kindness and self-transcendence.

This metaphor does not mean dealing with heavy burdens or some horrible things that life has thrown our way. What kind of a God would require such dreadful sacrifice? To take up your cross is to take up that burden of *learning to surrender your will to God,* because isn't that exactly what Jesus did in the Garden of Gethsemane when he was about to literally take up the cross? *"Not my will but yours!"*

We need help from the Holy One, and until we accept that, we can't take up that cross of letting go of our willfulness, of surrendering ourselves into God's will, of accepting what might seem unacceptable in the name of God. It's called spiritual work, inner work, spiritual warfare within, and it takes place every moment of every day. It can give your life meaning and purpose, it can fill you with zeal, and it can lead you into the joy of the Master.

The third teaching to his disciples is: *"Follow me."* Now we've heard about "followers" over the years, especially during the 1970s in relation to cults, and the idea of mindless sheep checking their brains in at the door. Yet, even so, those who pursued those kinds of teachers were desperate for something. They were looking for spiritual meaning in a materialistic world.

Be sure that this is not what Jesus is talking about when he speaks of our becoming "followers." In fact, that's not even the word he uses. In the Greek, he does not say *"follow me,"* but rather, *"come after me,"* meaning *enter into my way of life, live out my way of being in the world.* Notice that when you understand that term *"come after me"* as one of the three key cornerstones of being Christian, it calls us to align ourselves with the right position in life – to forgive our enemies, to love those who hurt you, and to do all those things that the natural self is not interested in at all.

We often try to re-craft what it means to be a disciple, and we become like Peter, wanting to do it our way instead of

Christ's way. The cosmic requirement is always the same: *"Get behind me and walk the way I am leading."* Originally, Christians were called People of the Way. This kind of inner transformation is so personal and so immediate, that every decision and every choice you make from moment to moment, is caught in these teachings: Deny yourself; take up your cross; and come after me. The purpose is not to live some kind of dark and unhappy life, but to be liberated from the captivity of the self-absorbed life.

We are then told – *What good does it do to gain the whole world and lose your life.* In Greek, the word for life translates as "soul." He is talking about losing or selling out your soul. He is talking about betraying the core of yourself for material things and for the way of the world. How many of us have had to deal with this? He does not call us this way for our unhappiness and restriction, but for their very opposites. The Anointed One calls us to this way of life for the joy and bliss and liberty of living fully in the presence of God each and every day and every moment.

6

Faith

In order to understand how powerful this teaching is, we must first realize what the disciples had just been told after crying out *"Increase our faith!"* Here are the people who have left everything to follow the Anointed One, and who have given up on everything except for him. They have gone all the way, and yet they are saying *"Increase our faith."* Why do they say that?

Jesus has just told them that they must forgive seven times, and in another scripture, seventy times seven. The number seven is a symbol from mystic Hebrew numerology, as exemplified in Genesis, in reference to God creating the world in seven days. It was never meant to be understood literally. Seven is the number of perfection, the number of God, so Jesus is saying "take perfection, square it to infinity, and that's how often we are to forgive." This is why these men and women of God cry out in despair for an increase in faith. They know that such capacity for forgiveness is seemingly impossible.

The Greek word for forgiveness is *atheime,* which means to let go, to put down the baggage and move on, to not let the damage of the past continue to damage you. This teaching liberates you, as well as the other person. And these disciples, who have left everything, who have gone all the way and beyond, know they cannot do that. Then comes the real teaching in response to the request *"increase our faith,"* or *"enable us to do this impossible thing in our hearts and souls."*

Jesus begins by saying: *"If you had any faith..."* Notice he doesn't say, *If you had just a little faith.* No, he is saying, *If you had any faith at all!* Jesus is talking about a different kind of faith, not just a belief system, not just adherence to a doctrine, but something else that enables us to do the impossible. He then gives us a bizarre picture of how that with faith, we would tell a mulberry tree to be uprooted and planted in the ocean, and it would obey.

In French, the translation is: "uproot yourself." Uproot yourself and go plant yourself in the ocean. What does this symbolize? This is a picture of the utterly impossible. Jesus says that faith is an empowerment that enables you to do precisely what you think you cannot do right now – in other words, it is a different kind of faith. Faith is not about thinking a certain way or not thinking a certain way.

You can do the impossible, and live a transfigured, transformed, transcendent existence of the best of who you are. You can be Christ-like in this world and save yourself and others from misery and despair. Now that kind of faith, which isn't just following or believing, is a way of being that goes beyond the rational thought injected into us by our culture. That kind of faith opens onto a higher level that enables us to look at the world around us and see more than just what the senses see.

If we do not open ourselves up mentally, emotionally, and physically to that which is vaster and greater than we are, we don't know what faith is yet. This is the nuclear power of spiritual vision handed down through time, and available to us to change our life right now. When you see the world through eyes of faith, God is in it, not just in your mind, but in the experience. You *are* no longer. Jesus did not come to explain everything to us, but to give us the means of living differently.

Some folks spell faith R-I-S-K, because we have to be vulnerable, sensitive, courageous, and willing to go beyond what we think we know in order to enter into that Presence of God, which does indeed make all things new. This is all about *experience.* The trouble with external religion is that it reduces the teachings to commands and laws, and takes away the glorious experience of personal transformation into becoming a better person because you have opened yourself. The Greek word for faith is *pistis*, which means *to make obey.* To make all the different parts of ourselves obey that which is the most precious, the most beautiful, the most important.

When Jesus says about the disciples, "You faithless and perverse generation," that word perverse *means turning in all directions*, not having a polar star, not having a sense of which way to go. The power of faith, that new experience of life, unifies us with what we choose to do moment by moment and causes us to confront that part of us that wants nothing to do with these teachings. The greater part of ourselves is brought in line with that which is most important to us. That is spiritual warfare. It is the way we are called to walk; to turn everything in our life into an ability, a process to live out – the pain especially, as well as the joy, the surprises, the decisions and all of our situations of life, all of them feeding into that unified sense. It is a faith that leads us onwards.

These teachings end with a strange image of the master of the servant or slave, which is very first century. The servant does not sit down at the table with the master and eat. Such behavior would be considered an absurdity. It is difficult to relate to in our time, but the meaning is that as long as we live, we must never give up on the work of doing the will of our Master, no matter how often it falls on deaf ears, no matter how misunderstood we are! We must never give up on being and doing good. Don't ever think: "I've done all, I quit. Nobody says 'thank you' to me; no one listens; and no one cares." Jesus teaches us to keep doing what God wants us to be doing. Live to please God in what you are doing always and everywhere, no matter what. That is not a harsh commandment, but rather, the way to joy and peace.

7

Rebirth

This teaching may well include some of the most important words Jesus ever spoke. It is the axis of his teaching, the purpose of his ministry and the revelation he brings to each of us. We must put aside what we think we know about these metaphors that we have heard so often, and we must go deeper.

Nicodemus, a Pharisee – that is, a religious person with discipline and belief in the Holy – comes to Jesus at night. He had to come *at night.* Many of us have come to Jesus at night when no one is looking because it is politically incorrect nowadays to hold these beliefs. We live in troubled times, and some of us do not want to be called Christians because of our fear that others will mock us and not understand us, or think we are unintelligent. So we often come to spiritual teaching at night because it isn't the way of the culture. We live in a culture where materialism is king. It's the "show me" state of mind – "If I don't see it, I don't believe in it; if I can't touch it, it's not real." Some have called it *the superstition of materialism.* We absorb the belief that our little three dimensional box of the senses is all there is, regardless of the wondrous and mysterious universe surrounding us. And so we come to Jesus at night.

Nicodemus, the religious person, says: *"Teacher, you must be sent from God because of all these things you do."* Jesus answered him even though he didn't ask a question. Nicodemus believes a certain way. It's not that he is an unbeliever, but he believes because of the external miracles.

Jesus responds: *"Very truly,"* or, *"verily, verily..."* according to most translations. The actual words are: *"Amen, amen! No one sees the kingdom of God unless he or she is born from above."* No one. We have to understand what this means. *The kingdom of God* is a metaphor for the Presence of God – eternity in time. The other metaphor, *born from above*, has been grossly misrepresented. To be born again is not an instant event, nor is it a belief system. It is that process of going from who you once were, or who you are now, to the spiritual being that God calls you to be.

The things of this world, our psychology, our opinions and our behaviors, are all implied in the term "flesh is flesh." Nicodemus says: *"I'm an old man, how can I be born again?"* And then he says the most absurd thing: *"How can I re-enter the mother's womb?"* This is a perfect illustration of literal thinking and literal reading of Scripture. It is called Holy Scripture because you must go deeper, or else you will end up like Nicodemus, in complete confusion.

Being "born from above" means to have conscious awareness of God, of the sacred, of the holy in the midst of daily life. It means being cleansed of the mistakes, of the knots and wounds that life has inflicted upon you, and of the wrong thinking in which your culture and your parents and the media have buried you alive. It means to have a whole new perspective on existence, not tied to the ways of this world, to your personality, or to your attitudes.

Our identity is tied to our jobs, our nationalities, our parents, and even the movies we watch, all telling us what a man and a woman must be. All of these things are blown out of the water in this new understanding and perspective called "born from above" – you are seeing and living in a new way. It is radical. It is dynamic. This is transforming metamorphosis like the caterpillar to the butterfly. It's not about *not being you*, it's about becoming the *you* that you were always supposed to be. It is entering into the glorious freedom of the children of God.

We must begin to think differently and this is a process, a journey. It is a "fall down and get up again" effort. Out of the energy and Presence and life of God, we can be awakened to a new self, a deeper self, a true self; one that hasn't been hammered by life, broken down, full of depression and hopelessness, and all those ungodly things which salvation is meant to free us from.

But in order to obtain all this, you have to die to that old self. You have to fight against that old way and know that something new awaits. Jesus says to Nicodemus: *"You are Israel's teacher and you don't understand these things?" "You are an elder of the church and you don't understand these things?"* Jesus always challenges us, always takes us back to the beginning to learn again.

Then he speaks these strange words: *"Just as Moses lifted up…"* referring to an ancient story from the book of Numbers, where the Israelites were complaining. They would rather go back to their masters in Egypt who treated them cruelly, but with whom they were familiar, than to go forward into the unknown. They were surrounded by poisonous snakes, and many of the people of Israel died, so they came to Moses seeking forgiveness, saying these poisonous snakes of anger, resentment, intolerance and unforgiveness are killing us little by little. Moses raised the bronze serpent staff which represented the judgment of God, and told them that all they had to do was to look at it.

All you have to do, says God, is look at this teaching from the Anointed One. Hear his words and you will be freed. You will be brought back to life from all the rigid things that keep you narrow and cold, instead of alive in spirit.

The Israelites were willing to cut their losses and let those who had been bitten die, as long as the others could be saved. But, once again, God gives us more than we could hope for. Even the ones who were done for, however far they were from faith, were told that all they had to do was look....all *you* have to do is look to the Truth of the teaching and revelation. Fix your eyes on the Holy One who was brought into this world to take you out of your mess, to help you enter that new life in God which makes you a light in this world.

8

Facing the Storms

This is a teaching on how we can bring God into our storms, our problems. This is not a story from long ago. It's not about how wonderful Jesus is. This is nothing less than Jesus telling us how we, today, in our personal issues, can bring God's power into our lives. It is holy revelation, Holy Scripture.

Jesus is telling his disciples that they're going to cross the Sea of Galilee. We are told that it was evening. Professional fisherman knew that the Sea of Galilee was six hundred and eighty feet below sea level and that in the evening a funnel of hot and cold air was generated that made storms a certainty. So Jesus was saying: *"Let's go off into the storm together…Let's cross to the other side."* Let's cross to the other side of how we've always lived. Let's cross to the other side of how you behave without God. Let's look at life differently, from another view.

Jesus is always trying to get us to go to the other side, away from what is comfortable. We can easily dock our boats and stay as we always have been, but Jesus is revealing to us here in this scripture that we are called to go with him through the storm to the other side, into the unknown, into what seems dangerous to everyone else. So go to the other side of your impatience, go to the other side of your unforgiveness, your anger, your resentment, your fear and your unbelief. Go to the other side of how you take life. This is the call. The meaning and purpose of this teaching is to get us to become the God-centered people we are meant to be. You'll notice that you may have to leave the crowd behind, because most people do not want to do this. So you must leave the crowd and do it alone. Most of you know by now that there is going to be a storm in your life. You win the lotto, then you get cancer. You have a great job, then the economy falls. All kinds of things happen as life keeps moving. Life is change, and we don't like change, but we must learn to weather the storms.

Those storms are not just out there, but within as well, in our own emotional pain. Notice how the storm is described. The boat was swamped. You are swamped with your emotions, your fears and your uncertainties. But they had the Anointed One in the boat. They took Jesus with them. You've got to have the Holy One in your boat.

What does it mean to have Jesus in your boat? Are you remembering God in a difficult circumstance? How about the last time you were filled with rage, did you say to yourself: *"I don't want to go down that road again. I know where that leads."* Most of the time, we cannot do this unless we remember who is in our boat...that Jesus is in our boat with us, that God is present, and help is near. This knowing will invoke spiritual power into your situation. It will lift you out of what you cannot do by yourself. This is powerful, life changing teaching for right here and now.

So here comes that storm, and Jesus is asleep in the boat. This means two things. First, it represents the dark night of the soul, when you can't find God anywhere, and feel abandoned by God. The great teachers of our faith tell us that the dark night of the soul is full of unanswered prayers. Where is God? Why aren't you helping me? Is there a God? That dark night of the soul can lead you to more powerful faith. It is not a dead end, it is a growth process. So when you think that God is asleep in your boat and everything is falling apart, be sure that is not the case. This teaching is to tell us very clearly that we are never abandoned, we are never separated. All you have to do is remember that he is in the boat and that he cares about the minute things of your life. He knew you before you were born and he journeys with you through this life. And he knows you cannot do it by yourself.

What else does it mean that he is asleep? In the midst of this giant storm with violence all around, everyone is scared to death. Yet Jesus is at peace, supremely confident. Jesus knows the end of the story. Jesus knows who's in charge. Jesus knows God is good, and he can be at peace through the nightmare. We are called to that kind of peace. It is possible for us. It is not for a supernatural being; it is not only for saints; the metaphor is intended for you and me in our specific circumstances. It is for us to know that we can have such peace in the midst of insanity, that we are able to rest through the storm. So how do we do that? The Bible is full of answers, but the poor disciples, being just like us, are crying out: *"Lord, teacher, don't you care that we are dying? Are you not anxious?"*

When you're worried, upset or angry, and in the presence of someone who is not feeling that way, do you ever have the feeling of *what's wrong with you? Don't you feel my pain? Don't you care about me? I'm all upset, why aren't you upset? Let's all be upset together.* People like to share their upsetness. It feels good. That's the ungodly way. But Jesus is the non-anxious presence. He is the presence of certainty that *God is*, which makes no sense to human beings. We like to dwell on things together, on negative things, on fearful things. We go to the movies together to be terrified, but we are called to become people who have true peace, not of ourselves, but because we know there is a God.

Jesus arises and rebukes the elements. The Greek *epitomia* means that he sizes up and firmly stills the adversary. In other words, he goes directly to the source of our trouble and silences it. God can silence our terror of cancer. God can silence our fear of life. God's power is such that all of our problems can be stilled. Our very mortality can be made non-frightening. The impossible can happen. So in an instant, all this violence, this terror, all the chaos of life is dead silent. The disciples are now more frightened of that phenomenon than they are of the storm. This is way out of their field of understanding. Utter stillness. Utter calm.

When you are out of control internally with your storm of life, remember Jesus saying *peace, be still* and let God do it for you. Let God quiet your emotions. You know what happens when you let yourself fly off the handle. You know the disaster and destruction that come your way – what utter darkness invades you. Anything can happen. And there is Jesus saying: *Peace, be still. I can control the source of your pain.* Someone once said: Don't tell God how big your problems are, tell your problems how big your God is! That leads to victorious living. That's what we are called to live each and every day.

After Jesus calmed the storm, the dead silence is unbelievable, unbearable in its unnaturalness, and so the disciples say: *"Who is this, who is this?"* We are not disconnected from God. God is not way out there somewhere. God is immediately present to us in our daily lives, and Jesus makes that real for us, not in a story book, not in an old miracle story, but in our life. This miracle for the disciples would never have happened had they stayed on shore, tied off the boat and taken it easy. In the easy and the familiar, there would have been no miracles in their lives. Our faith is spelled R-I-S-K. Risk what you don't know. Open yourself to the greater life that you do not know and cannot see, but that you can, like an infant, feel is surrounding you and loving you and caring for you every moment of your existence.

So Jesus further says to these people who are facing death in the storm: *"Why are you afraid?"* Isn't that a strange question? Jesus is asking us why we are afraid. It seems like the answer is simple – we are afraid of car wrecks, of burglary, of all the awful things of life. Of course we are afraid. The real teaching in Greek is *why are you cowards?* Have you still no faith? In Mark 4:11, he has just told them and us: *"To you has been given the secret of the kingdom of God, the secret of experiencing God in this life,"* and yet here they are, cowards again. So he's calling all of us, challenging us to step into that faith that does not feel the deadly storm. Because if we're not in faith, and we're in fear, there is no God present.

If we're overwhelmed by fear, we cannot get in touch with God. The faith part lifts us into God's presence and power, and brings it into our lives, so Jesus makes no bones about it. *"Why are you cowards? What are you waiting for? Wake up. I'm in the boat. I will save you."* This is for each of us who choose to believe that God is real, that all things can be dealt with, that we're not alone, and that the Anointed One is in our boat and will still off all the storms.

9

Signs

"I've come to bring fire. Do you think I've come to bring peace? No." You must agree that this statement in Luke is not the Jesus you usually think about. The parallel passage in Matthew is *"I've come to bring division…. I've come to bring a sword."* This does not fit with our idea of Jesus. We have to understand what is being said here, because it is so radically outside of our image of the Prince of Peace.

Can you imagine how shocking this would be in the first century when family was not merely the natural unity, but also your identity, your security, your direction and your purpose? Without family, there was nothing in society to take part in. And here is Jesus at his most radical, saying these shocking words. We are supposed to be shocked. And in that state of shock perhaps our mind opens up just a little more to something we haven't thought about when it comes to the teaching, the presence and the purpose of the Anointed One.

We have to be knocked out of our box, out of our comfort zone. How easy it is to go to sleep and forget that he walked to the cross, not to make us comfortable, but to renew our lives – to call us into a new way of life here, today. *"I have come to bring fire."* Let's not take it literally. He is not trying to cause the apocalypse, but it is something dramatic that we've got to grasp.

Fire is used over 450 times in the Bible as a metaphor of God's Presence and power. The great prophets spoke of it. Elijah cried out: *"If I'm a man of God, bring fire down from heaven against the prophets of Baal!"* Or Isaiah saying that God's tongue is a devouring fire. Malachi, the last prophet, in preparing the way for what was to come 400 years later, prophesied that on that day, we'll be burning like an oven and the evildoers will be stubble. John the Baptist talked about setting the ax to the root of the tree and throwing the trees that bear no fruit into the fire, and the baptism by fire of Holy Spirit. There are all these ideas, which could be reduced to judgment and wrath, but are really something so much more: Fire is the Power of God, the very Presence of God. *For our God is a consuming fire.....*

The Greek word for fire is *pur.* It is our word for pure. So fire means purification. Purification of who we are. Christ wants something within us to be purified, to be consumed for the creation of something new. In order to walk that path of understanding and of new life and purpose, something has to go. And if we don't know ourselves well enough yet, it's time, under these radical teachings, to pay attention. It is not easy to live out these teachings, because they require a new way of life, a godly way of life, an enlightened way of life.

In seeking to heal each of us individually, Jesus is giving the world a chance to heal completely, one person at a time. This is not generic. This is very much for each human being. So take a situation from this week where you forgot about God, where you did not behave the way you would have liked, where you were just lost in yourself, in your habits and your behavior. Now bring these words to mind: *"I have come to bring fire and division."* Jesus is saying *come out from that old way of behaving. Come out from among them and be purified.*

We have to recognize how big a job we are facing. Take that example of the family. Surely, you know that just as he doesn't want to set the forest on fire, neither does he want to destroy the nucleus of the family. He is making a point here that our belief in God's call on our life is far superior in allegiance to our greatest allegiance on earth – that of our blood ties with family which are unquestionable, most of the time. Jesus is saying that beyond this great priority, is our priority for God.

Evelyn Underhill, one of the great scholars of Christian teaching in the twentieth century, wrote wonderful books on Christian spirituality. Here was a little English lady who made a great impact on the world that continues even to this day. Yet, both her husband and son were unbelievers. So here was a woman full of the legacy of Christianity, who shared with the world these methods of awakening to God, yet she could not share them in her kitchen or living room.

These truths are not passed on from family to family or from tribe to tribe. They are passed on one individual at a time, from one person who wakes up and whose spirit understands this truth. One person who says, "this is what I'm committing myself to even if it goes against the norm, against the accepted, not just with family, but with the whole culture." Our entire modern culture now finds it politically incorrect to be Christian.

It is not about ideals, not about a belief system. It is about how you're going to live and behave in the simplest moments of life. We are called to that painful and dramatic decision because something has to be consumed and purified within us. What is it? It's that selfishness. It's those imitations of our parents. It's whatever interferes with our being a whole person – a child of God fully functional and able to possess the strength of character to forgive or to say *no* when it is necessary. That's not easy. That wasn't easy in seventh grade, it is not easy as an adult, and that's what Jesus is calling us to. He says, *"How I yearn…"* Down through time Christ's spirit is yearning that each one of us be on fire for God, be on fire for good, be on fire for living, as we are all called to live above the conflict and violence that is all around us.

Jesus tells us that he has a "baptism to undergo." It isn't baptism with water. It is the baptism of suffering. The suffering that brings about change. The word means "immersed and overwhelmed," and it refers to that walk to the cross. He says: *"How much distress I am in until it is accomplished."* That's a translation. We hear the word *stress*, and I doubt that Jesus used the word stress in the first century. What he was saying is, *how I long for that goal to be accomplished, how I want to be consecrated so that each person in the world can see that God has broken into time, and reached out to each of us.*

But the masses do what can be expected of human behavior, and refuse to make that radical choice of living in a self-transcendent way. The prophet Micah cries out: "*The faithful have disappeared from the land and there is no one left who is upright. Your enemies are members of your own household.*"

What intuition is necessary to know that goodness is at the heart of the universe? What kind of courage does it take to stand on your beliefs – to stand on your certainty that God exists despite what people think? It takes tremendous courage. There is nothing like peer pressure or family pressure. So I encourage you to be strong and to accept that loneliness which necessarily comes when you know that you must be the black sheep. How often must we bring to our remembrance the words of Jesus, *"If they persecuted me, they will persecute you."* For what are you persecuted? For believing in goodness at the heart of reality. Don't be afraid to be the only one to say, like Martin Luther, *"Here I stand, I can do no more."*

As long as there exists a handful of people on this planet who will take that stand, there is hope for humanity. This is why that in this segment of verses, we find Jesus referring to the *signs of the times*, and makes the reference to seeing a cloud in the west. In those lands, to the west was the Mediterranean, so everyone knew that clouds coming from the west meant rain from the ocean. Winds from the south meant that the desert winds were coming through and it would be scorching hot. These obvious things were so much a part of the lives of the people, yet they missed the important signs – the spiritual signs of the present times. This is for us today. He calls us hypocrites. We, who believe there is a God, and yet don't see what is going on. We don't see the disintegration of society and civilization, the thirty, forty and fifty-year long migration out of the churches.

The world is in trouble. Values are freefalling. Some years ago, when profanity on television was first allowed, the first one to be used, was to take the Lord's name in vain. This was an aggressive rejection of that which is Holy, of that which is sacred, of that which has held the best of humanity together. So Jesus cries out to each of us: *Don't you see the signs of the times? Don't you understand what this means?* It means we can't stick to the status quo, to the way it has always been, because today is a new day, a troubled day.

There are at least two generations of people who haven't been in church, who are hungry for some kind of meaning in a meaningless world.

We are called today to take responsibility for what we believe in, to have our hearts filled with that fire that Christ longed for in every human being. It is your calling to be a dwelling place for the Holy, and nothing less. Let us then be purified of all that keeps us from fulfilling that calling.

10

Who is He?

We are told that Jesus went near to Caesarea Philippi, by the foot of Mount Hermon, near one of the main sources of the River Jordan. Why is this meaningful? Why is this geography in the Holy Scripture? Strangely enough, it is because he is in Gentile territory to make his revelation as the Anointed One. This tells us that he came for all people. He came for humanity. And in this announcement, he is already outside the bounds of the religion of this time. He is here for all to understand, each in our own way, what this means.

It has been some time now that he has been on the road with his disciples, and he asks them the question: *"Who do people say that I am?"* We hear from the disciples that they think he might be Elijah reincarnated, resurrected. Why Elijah? At the end of the Old Testament, on the very last page in the Book of Malachi, there are mysterious words of Elijah coming in the future, *on the day of the Lord* – the Day of Judgment, the day when every human being comes before their Maker, their conscience and their destiny. Malachi prophesizes: *"You see, I will send you the prophet Elijah before that grave and dreadful day of the Lord."*

The disciples realize that Jesus is so significant, so much more than a prophet, that he may be that prophet of the end times, the one revealing God's judgment to the world. Others, knowing that he is not your average rabbi, say that he is John the Baptist returned from the dead. King Herod himself was scared to death that this powerful spiritual man was going to come back and haunt him, make him pay for his awful deeds.

Some say that the holy man from Nazareth is Jeremiah. Why Jeremiah? Jeremiah, uniquely, was the prophet of the inner life, of lamentation and crying for the people, the prophet of the mystical awareness of God. We know one thing – Jesus called himself *Son of Man.* Eighty times in the gospel, we hear that strange term *son of man.* What does son of man mean? Son of humanity, perhaps. But Jesus used that term on purpose, because no one knew what it meant.

No one was quite sure who he was, and he could not be pigeon holed, not even to this day. We find the term *son of man* in the vision of Daniel: *"In my vision at night, I looked and there before me was one like a son of man. Coming with the clouds of heaven, he approached the Ancient of Days and was led into His presence. He was given authority, glory, sovereign power, over all people and nations. Men of every language worshiped him and his dominion is an everlasting one and his kingdom one that will never be destroyed."*

Jesus then asks: *"Who do you say that I am?"* and that *you* is plural. He is not addressing Peter, but each of us right now. *Who do you say that I am?* That is the eternal question. It is the ultimate question, because our answer to that question changes everything in our lives. And so Peter takes a chance and cries out: *"You are the Christ, the Son of the living God!"* No one had ever said those words before in human history: *You are the Christ, the Anointed One, the Messiah.*

Jesus says: *"Blessed are you..."* because he knows that this is an understanding of who he is. It is not a deduction, an analysis or a logical or philosophical statement. It is spirit revealed. It is the moment when the old fisherman breaks out of all his boxes and sees before him the Eternal in time, God's Presence incarnated in the world – *Emmanuel*, God among us, the Logos. Then Christ further says, *"no one has revealed this to you."* It is after this that Jesus states: *"you are Peter and on this rock, I will build my church."*

What confusion came from that! From those words comes the Catholic Church, the Pope, then all of the fragmentations of the Faith that have come into existence since then. But in the Greek, he says: "you are *Petros*," the masculine for *stone*. You are the stone, and on this *petra*, feminine for bedrock, I will build my church. In other words, the Church is not built on Peter the man, but on the recognition of who Christ is and the implications of how that changes each one's way of life.

Christ builds his church on every one who has that wisdom and understanding. And when he says "my church," it is the only time in the Gospel that we see those words: "my *ecclesia*"...my assembly of those who are called out. So it is not the Presbyterian Church, the Methodist Church, the Baptist Church, your church or my church; it is *his* church. It is a living organism made up of people who have been called together and who understand what it means that Christ is the Anointed One of God.

How do we understand this? How do we connect the Son of man and Messiah, or the Anointed One of God? Between the Greek philosophers talking about substance and person, "truly human, truly divine," down to the nineteenth century, and the rational search for the historical Jesus, there is no end to the complications. Those are not the paths to understanding Jesus. It is necessary to awaken to a new consciousness of what this means.

If Christ is the Son of the living God, it means that in the human being that he was, the full consciousness of God was present. There is a quality of consciousness that comes to us in a moment of great fear or gratitude, or from *being still,* which lifts us beyond our ordinary perceptions and into a state where we are intensely aware of everything around us. This is what it means to exist in the present, and this is the state Christ was in at all times. It is where God *is.* Christ is the model of where we can be in terms of awakening to this existence.

There are many kinds of philosophers, prophets, and holy men and women in the world. Then, there is that ultimate manifestation in human form of a quality of being that can only be called mercy incarnate, or compassion incarnate. When you and I recognize that this is the ultimate direction, then our lives can no longer be the same. We understand that mature life is meant to be the full consciousness of God, the full presence of goodness in the world.

Jesus did not come here to be worshipped, he came to enable our personal transformation. He shows us who we are called to be, each in our own way, in every little detail of life. We know within ourselves when we begin to get less aware of God. In those moments of rage, or shutting down, or not being willing to understand another, we are far from God. It is then that we must remember who we are meant to be. If this is who Jesus is, then this is who I must become.

Jesus goes on to say: *"I will give you the keys of the kingdom that you may bind and you may loose."* These are rabbinic terms about what is forbidden and what is correct about opening the scrolls and teaching rightly. In other words, it is the promise that teachers will continually be raised up so these timeless Truths shall be made known to all generations.

11

Persistence

We have before us a crucial teaching. At the request of the disciple, *"Lord, teach us to pray,"* the Lord's Prayer itself is a teaching that informs us how we are to communicate with God, with the sacred, and how we go from our ordinary selves to encounter the holy, the unknown, the mysterious and the invincible. It is the relationship to spirit, to *Holy Spirit.* It is the invoking of the power and activity of God into our lives.

So we need to know what Jesus is telling us here. He says: "*When you pray, go into the secret place and the Father who hears in secret will hear you.*" Now what do you think that means? He is telling us that we cannot reach God, we cannot connect directly with Spirit from the superficial, from the false, from the phony, from the show, from the personality that we put forth in our daily life. We have to go where nobody is looking. We have to go to that intimate, private place that is real. It is from the real that we connect with the Real, which is why when we're running on automatic, nothing can happen.

Now let's deal with that word "Father." Even in ancient civilizations, they used the word "Father" to speak of the Creator of the universe. There is an ancient hymn to the moon God saying "You who hold the life of all things in your hands..." So even then, that word *father* contained the motherly element of nurture and care. God is neither male nor female, so don't let that word get in the way. But notice this other word appended to the full prayer – *Our* Father – yours, mine. When we say *our* Father, we are instantly connected. What keeps us as separate people is our self-love, our ego, our illusions and our fears. In the real world, we are all connected; we are all part of that one source which we recognize as revealed by the Christ himself. We are not isolated and alone. We are brothers and sisters, truly. We are part of something greater than ourselves.

"Who art in heaven..." This is a means of transmission, a way to get a message to a higher world, and nothing less. Jesus is giving us a methodology. We cannot do it out of habit, and we have to know what to pray for.

God knows what we need, and we are given analogies to illustrate the point of prayer. There is the parable of one who has gone to bed, when a friend comes late at night asking for loaves to set before a guest; and another of a widow who seeks a judge to avenge her of an adversary. In each analogy, due to their persistence, the requests of both are granted and they receive what they are asking. This does not mean that God is not interested, or that there is reluctance from the Spirit to respond. What this analogy means is that it is difficult to get through to such a deeply profound other place, and we must therefore persist, just as those examples demonstrate.

The word persistence in Greek means *shameless impudence.* Jesus is saying that you have to be shamelessly asking, knocking, seeking, and never giving up. That's what it takes. That's what Jesus said about prayer, about contact with Spirit. We have to have such faith that nothing will be an obstacle to connecting with that grace of God which is available. Think of what must be cleared out of the way for this to take place. Imagine what courage, what persistence it takes to stand in faith in the face of illness and setbacks, confusion, tragedies, and all the issues of life.

Thy will be done on earth as it is in heaven. Let's put to rest once and for all the silly argument of the atheist that there can be no God because of all the terrible things that go on. Don't you know that all those awful things go on because of people, not because of God? God's will is not done on earth. People's greed and violence are what create the horrors of this world. Do you know we've got enough money to feed all the children of the world, but we're doing something else with it? "*Thy will be done on earth*" has to begin with your earth, in your life, in your world. That's how God's will enters the world.

Give us this day our daily bread. Do you know that the word *daily* is not the word in the original text? We keep translating it daily bread and so we keep saying it. The Greek is *epiousio*, – give us that which is our own from above. The Aramaic is *mahar*, the bread of tomorrow. Not Monday's bread but the final tomorrow, the great completion of life, the fullness of time, the appearance of God in our reality. Give us that which is to feed our spirit. Give us spiritual understanding to make it through another day, spiritual wisdom for the moment, and for the circumstances in which we find ourselves.

Forgive us our sins. Jesus is revealing to us a powerful cosmic Truth here. We cannot be forgiven if we don't forgive. God, the Creator of all things, cannot forgive us if we stay locked in our unforgiveness. He cannot get through to us until we have forgiven. It's cosmic mathematics. The same channel that brings us mercy is the channel from which we have released mercy.

Next time you have occasion to say that prayer – "as we forgive those who have sinned against us" – put a face on it. Put that person who you do not want to forgive in your consciousness and if you do that, if you dare to forgive in that moment of asking for forgiveness, you will know God's grace. You will find liberation and release. It works. We just have to use it right. If we're just babbling along not meaning it and not forgiving while we say so, too bad for us. We have missed our opportunity.

Then, there are these strange words: *"Lead us not into temptation."* In the Letter of James, Jesus' brother, we have something to the effect that no one should say that God tempts them because God tempts no one. It is not God who is tempting us. These words are saying, *Lord when the hour of temptation comes, help me to not succumb. Walk with me. Carry me through it.*

Another saying of Jesus that comes from the Gospel of Thomas is: *No one can obtain the kingdom of heaven if he or she does not go through temptation.* These are the temptations of conceit, pride and self-righteousness – all the things that cut us off from God.

Now what builds your muscles is the opposition you encounter in the process of temptation. If you grow a plant in a green house, it will be very luscious and beautiful, yet because it never experienced wind and storms, it's going to be too weak to resist the weather. Have you seen the trees along the coast that have been battered for decades? They are twisted, crooked things, but they're still standing. Making the right choices strengthens your faith and develops true character. We have to walk through it. We're asking God to be with us as we walk through it so we don't break.

This Prayer, given to us by the Anointed One himself, is on fire with Christ's spirit and wisdom, and is designed specifically to lead us into encounter with God – to bring God fully into our lives, and to break down the walls between us and God.

12

Salvation

Most of us know the story of Zacchaeus up in that sycamore tree. We learned it in Sunday school, read the story, complete with cartoon figures, and even sang the silly little song about it, yet this is a mighty teaching. It is divine wisdom for each of us on the transforming power of gratitude for being accepted. So take another look at this ancient teaching and discover what it is that is being offered to you. Let's begin with setting the context.

Jesus comes into Jericho. Now that's significant, because Jericho is approximately 17 miles northeast of Jerusalem, and was the city that connected to the east, the lands of Syria, Asia Minor, Babylon and Persia. It was at the junction of several trading routes, so all the incoming merchandise came through Jericho on oriental spice caravans, camels and donkeys. It is against this backdrop that our prototype is pictured in one Zacchaeus: the tax collector.

Zacchaeus was a collaborator. This word was used in France during World War II. "Collaborator." It is someone who betrays others by working with the enemy, with the invaders against his own people. That's who Zacchaeus was. He was collecting burdensome taxes from the people for the Romans, and was hated and reviled. He was considered as low as a murderer, thief or prostitute. He was totally rejected by his community, but was very rich, very important and very frightening, because he was not just a tax collector, friend of the brutal Romans, he was *chief* tax collector. He got a piece of the action from all the other tax collectors.

What does that have to do with you and me? We have here the figure of somebody who is so hopelessly godless, so full evil, self-interest, and wrongdoing, that you couldn't get any farther from the holy and the pure. Isn't it interesting that this ungodly kind of character wants to see this holy man from the Galilean hill country? Why would someone who has essentially given up on being incorporated into the community and into the religion of his ancestors, want to see the prophet from Nazareth? Yet this man who is rejected by religious people, who seems utterly lost, and who is not deemed to be worth saving, somehow senses there is something different about this new and mighty prophet. Don't you know that we are all like Zacchaeus, hopelessly lost in our imperfections? We are all in that boat, and yet something about this revelation of divine compassion through the Anointed One tells us that we're accepted anyway.

So it's no longer about Zacchaeus...now it's about you. *You* are accepted in your limitations, your imperfections, your mistakes, and your sinfulness. In spite of everything, the Uncreated One has come for you, loves you, and is looking for you. Is there any greater reason to be grateful?

This is our story. And what do we find here? Zacchaeus has to struggle through the crowd. He cannot see, get to, experience or understand the Holy without doing so. Once again, we have obstacles to overcome. Not only our internal ones – our own selfishness and lack of desire to be compassionate, merciful, and to believe in something greater than ourselves – but those external ones too. We must persist in spite of our whole culture, which dissuades us and interferes with our spiritual effort. Even some churches keep us from seeing Jesus as well. You could be rationalistic about it and say *okay, Zacchaeus is a short guy. He's got to climb up high to see.* Or, you could bring it home to yourself and make it very personal and spiritual: All of us are short and all of us small when it comes to understanding the deep things of the spirit or attempting to grasp what this God idea is, and how to live it out. All of us are shortsighted. All of us are limited. And so he climbs the tree. And in the Middle East, even to this day, it is unseemly and undignified for a man of means to be seen running. Yet here is the wealthiest man in town, covered in jewels, doing the undignified thing of climbing a tree. What does that tell us? He is desperate. He will do anything. He will endure mockery. He doesn't care what the hundreds of people who already hate him are going to think. Sometimes you have to not care what people think in order to "see" or understand a new spiritual perspective, and this takes courage.

So this man, rejected by all of society for good reasons, is up in that tree. The righteous people have good reason to find him unworthy. But what happens next? Jesus comes by and calls out: *"Zacchaeus!"* How did Jesus know his name? This teaching tell us that he knows your name. God knows your name. You may not know God, but God knows your name. That's a shocking revelation. Nobody in the crowd whispered it to him; Jesus knew that child of God, and knows *you* as child of God too.

He tells him to come down from that tree: "I must go to your house today." The Greek word means "*it is necessary for me to go to your house today.*" And what does that mean? It means that Jesus didn't come through Jericho by accident, he didn't run into Zacchaeus by mistake, and this was no coincidence. Rather, it is a timeless moment in which humanity is taught for all time why we ought to live in gratitude. This event *had* to be. This was designed so that you, in this time, can understand what the revelation is – that the Holy has come for you too, whatever your limitations are. *I must come to your home today.* You, the last person imaginable.

This is an example of the divine way: God accepts us and we change. The human way is: "You'd better say you're sorry and then maybe I'll forgive you." We don't accept until we get proper repentance. In the divine way, God loves and accepts us, and we respond because we are so filled with awe and gratitude to know that we are loved by the Heart of the Universe in spite of everything.

And what happens in this wonderful revelation that ought to bring joy and gratitude to every human being? People mutter and people grumble because they are unhappy with God's goodness. So Jesus comes to the house of the one man in town that a Holy Man would never go to in order to reveal divine love. Zacchaeus welcomes him gladly. That is the teaching: Welcoming such unconditional love gladly, not merely into your home, but into your heart. You cannot be grateful intellectually or philosophically. You've got to open your life, your soul, your psychology, your heart to the reality of Spirit, welcoming gladly that consciousness of acceptance and love.

Zacchaeus is so overwhelmed by this love of God manifested through the mercy and acceptance of the Anointed One in spite of everything he's done, that right then and there he becomes a different person. He gives half of his wealth away to whomever he has cheated. He gives four hundred fold. In the Torah, the sacred law, the Rabbis say that if you cheated somebody, you pay them back the restitution plus twenty percent. But this man – this every person who becomes aware of such Truth – is so grateful that he gives back four hundred percent. And he does this not to look good, but because his heart is so full. Then Jesus proclaims: "*Today salvation has come to this house!*"

In the midst of such transforming gratitude, the Anointed One gives us his mission statement: *"For the Son of Man has come to seek and save the lost."* He has come to seek out each of us in our lostness, our mistakes, our foolishness, our bad temper and our pettiness. He has come to seek us where we are and to wake us up to our Creator's love and acceptance, calling us out of that lostness and into a gratefulness that is conscious of the Presence of God, empowering us for the journey toward authentic transformation into our true potential. Such is the power of gratitude for the sacredness of Life. Such is the power of full, undeserved acceptance that embraces each one of us as a beloved child of the universe.

PART II

THE FRUITS OF THE JOURNEY

In the following section, the reader will find a variety of wisdom teachings which developed down through the centuries in the wake of the Anointed One's journey and revelations. Each chapter represents a period, from the first centuries to the Middle Ages and down to our era, tracing a spiritual awakening that transcends culture and time as a direct result of the Christ consciousness which incarnated into the world and has remained to this day as a door to new meaning and purpose for every person. We begin with an overview of the timeless insights on prayer, fully realized through the example of the Anointed One.

1

Deep Prayer
The Practice and Power of Spiritual Encounter

As a deer longs for flowing streams,
so my soul longs for you, O God.
My soul thirsts for God,
for the living God.
When shall I come and behold
the face of God?

Psalms 42:1, 2

The words of Jesus in the New Testament:

When you pray, do not keep on babbling like pagans for they think they will be heard because of their many words. Do not be like them for your father knows what you need before you ask him.

From Thomas Merton, a spiritual teacher in the twentieth century:

The only true joy on earth is to escape from the prism of our own false self and enter by love into union with the life who dwells and sings within the essence of every creature and in the core of our own souls.

Intimacy with God cannot be fully experienced without quietness of body, soul and spirit. An atmosphere of stillness is absolutely essential for the believer in Jesus if he or she is to enter into the experience of his deep communing love. In order for us to hear his still, small voice within us, we must become quiet.

Psalm 46:10 tells us: *Be still and know I am God.*

Other translations of that verse are *cease striving, let go, relax and know that I am God.* This knowing goes far beyond informational knowledge; it is to be *experienced,* and the experience comes only as a result of being still.

Our lives are in such a rush that often we miss the imperative of quieting ourselves as we approach God. We just run up to God, blurt out our prayers and rush away again. When we do this we will never fully enter into his presence. Psalm 37:7-8,11 sums it up this way: *Rest in the Lord, wait patiently for him to act.* Don't fret or worry; all who humble themselves before the Lord shall be given many blessings and shall have wonderful peace. As Jesus said: *My peace I give to you, my peace I leave with you.*

Quietness is not a new discovery or recent innovation. It's a time honored and proven method of having relationship with God that is almost totally ignored by modern day Christians. Contemplative prayer has been a part of the Christian teaching from the earliest days. This tradition was summed up by Saint Gregory the Great at the end of the sixth century. He called it *resting in God.* In this resting, the mind and heart are not so much asking or seeking God, but are beginning to experience, or to test what they have been seeking. This state is not the suspension of all activity, but the reduction of many acts and reflections into a single act or thought in order to sustain one's consent to God's presence and action.

This form of prayer was first practiced and taught by the desert fathers of Egypt, Palestine and Syria, including Evagrius, John Cassian and John Climacus, and has many representatives of every age – *in* every age. In the Patristic age it was Saint Augustine and Saint Gregory the Great in the West, and Pseudo-Dyonisius and the Hesychasts in the East.

In the middle ages, St. Bernard of Clairvaux, William of Saint Thierry, the Rhineland Mystics, one of them being Hildegard of Bigen, Meister Eckhart, Ruysbroec and Tauler.

And later it was the author of the Imitation of Christ, Thomas à Kempis, and the English Mystics of the fourteenth century, such as the anonymous author of the *Cloud of Unknowing;* Walter Hilton, Richard Rolle, and Julian of Norwich. Then, after the reformation, in the nineteenth century, it was the Carmelites, Teresa of Ávila, John of the Cross and Therese of Lisieux. Finally, among modern Christians are Thomas Merton, Basil Pennington, Thomas Keating and countless others, perhaps one of you. Some of you would be in that line of Christians who truly fall in love with God and have an unquenchable desire to be in God's presence.

Contemplative prayer is *alert receptivity* through consenting to God's presence and action within us, which places the emphasis on the purity of intention. It is not technique, it's not magic or special gifts, it is the purity of intention in our hearts that leads us into this wonder and mystery. According to John of the Cross, the purity of intention manifests itself during prayer as a *general loving attentiveness to God.* This attentiveness is not of the mind, but of the heart. Its source is pure faith in God's presence, leading to a surrender to the interior action of the Holy Spirit in the here and now.

For most people, ordinary life is characterized by the sense that God is absent. But if God were not present at every moment, we would not be here either. Creation is not a one time event, its God's ongoing gift on every level of our being from the tiniest quark in the subatomic world to the highest stages of consciousness. Teresa of Ávila wrote in the sixteenth century that all difficulties in prayer can be traced to one cause: *praying as if God were absent.*

This is the unfortunate conviction that we bring with us from early childhood and apply to everyday life and to our lives in general. It gets stronger as we grow up, unless we are touched by the gospel and begin the spiritual journey. This journey is a process of dismantling the *monumental illusion* that God is absent or even distant. When our particular requests and prayers are not answered, we become even more convinced that God is absent. The start, middle and end of the spiritual journey is the *conviction that God is always present.*

As we progress in this journey, we perceive God's presence more and more. If you seek God, you have a chance of finding God, and to move to a new level; to discover what you have always yearned for, but that after all these years you may have given up on. And now is a new opportunity. The spiritual journey is a gradual process of enlarging our emotional and mental relationship with the divine reality that is present in us, but not ordinarily accessible to our emotions and our mind.

Jesus is calling us to full human development, regrounding us in our source and enabling us to experience that this divine energy is infinitely tender, compassionate, nurturing, enabling and empowering. Jesus has experience of the Uncreated One as *Abba*, the God of infinite concern for every living thing, especially human beings. This is the great revelation that gives us new life. His experience of God was revolutionary in the religious context of his day. His understanding is reflected in the commentaries of the teachers of the church in every century. The divine indwelling is the truth of faith that is easily forgotten or avoided. It is the one on which a personal conversion radically depends.

The early church fathers called this process *the development of the spiritual senses.* The external senses perceive the immediacy of material reality. The spiritual senses perceive the immediacy of the divine reality in various forms by means of a gradual process in which the word of God is assimilated, interiorized and understood. As the process advances, the fruits of the spirit enumerated by Paul in Galatians 5, and by Jesus in the Beatitudes of Matthew 5, begin to emerge. These are signs that we are waking up to the divine presence.

The act of prayer has often been misunderstood and distorted to what it is not. Superficial piety, not to say superstition generally reduces prayer to a grocery list of needs and wants presented at times of trouble to some higher power that may or may not respond. In this kind of behavior there is no concept of change of self, of deeper insight into reality. It is true that the impulse behind the outcry for help is as instinctive as the need to stay near fire on a cold winter's night. But we are left with the emptiness of an individual calling out to a distant and unknown deity.

All religions have been carriers of this kind of prayer from the primitive tribal rights to the kneeling believer in a gothic cathedral. This fact alone ought to prove that we are dealing here with the most elemental, infantile form of prayer. In the evolution of humanity's spiritual awareness, we find that prayer becomes something very different. The great sages of all traditions reveal in their own lives that prayer is ultimately a uniting of human consciousness with the vaster life that they call divine.

We can therefore trace the development of prayer from petition – asking; to intercession – praying for others; to contemplation – silent transforming prayer. For the greatest spiritual visionaries, prayer emerges with breathing and moment to moment awareness. Consciousness of being alive becomes *intense receptivity of a higher reality.* Some traditions describe this state as *seeing the invisible in the visible.* This phenomenon is the end result of a lifetime of spiritual development, though every seeker can experience moments of illumination where mysterious joy or gratitude floods their heart. We are then lifted out of the mundane consciousness which we mistakenly take for reality, and experience the freedom, insight, and capacity to love that transcends our ordinary incarnations.

The transforming power of prayer deals with a more attuned awareness, an exalted consciousness of the present moment and a liberation from the psychological baggage that blocks our true identity. Consciousness is energy, and with a little discernment of our inner lives, we can easily notice the difference in quality in our various states. According to the great men and women of the inner life, prayer is *a response to the love of God for us.* They all point to the fact that prayer is ultimately a matter *of experiencing the presence of the transcendent.*

Prayer is meant to open our hearts to God by enabling us to surrender our inmost depths to the presence within us. According to the great men and women of the inner life, prayer is a response to feeling a love within us and around us, that lifts us up out of our troubles. In the experience of

Douglas Steel, a Quaker author, prayer is simply a form of waking up out of a dull sleep in which our life has been spent. He writes that in the most real prayer of all, there occurs a refocusing of our life until it is brought to abide in divine love. These were his words: "At those moments a man comes to recognize the distinction between his praying and his being prayed in...

"Unless you are ready and willing to seek that kind of inner empathy and submit to that kind of inner renovation, it would be better not to play at pray."

This texts remind us that we must put before all else, the universal commandment to remember God. Deuteronomy 7:18: *Thou shall love – thou shall remember the Lord thy God.*

Through the ancient tradition of the prayer of the heart, the Jesus prayer, one learns to pray always with every breath in every moment. But the first condition of any further development is for the beginner *to know himself or herself.* This means becoming aware of our *obstacles to communion with God.* This awareness of our bottomless presence leads to the disappearance of thoughts, and especially of our multiple desires. The great symbol of the ego, says Thomas Merton, is multiple desires which equal an ego of illusion that ought to be focused on *one great desire* which is to love God back.

This beginning point is common to all the great teachers of prayer. For the act of praying is not so much an effort on our part as it is *a manifestation and flowering of God's grace in us.* The purpose of human effort is to *clear away* the obstacles to this manifestation. We have been involved in the discovery of our true identity beneath the masks we wear and the defenses we have built up. In the process of dying to this artificial self, we can begin to live from a deeper center within, where the Eternal is encountered. This God consciousness is the essence of experiencing religion as transformation.

Thomas Kelly, another Quaker author, gives us a hint of what this new way of life implies:

"What is here urged are internal practices and habits of the mind. What is here urged are secret habits of unceasing orientation of the deeps of our being around the inward light. Ways of conducting our inward life so that we are perpetually bowed in worship where we are also busy in the world of daily affairs."

This practice is the heart of religion. Kelly further emphasizes the fact that at some point along the journey to this *becoming*, we discover that prayer is much more than technique, concentration and surrender:

"Although we begin the practice of secret prayer with a strong sense that we are initiators and that by our wills we are establishing our habits, maturing experience brings awareness of being met and tutored and purged and disciplined, simplified and made pliant in His holy will by a power waiting within us. For God himself works in our souls in their deepest depths taking increasing control as we are progressively willing to be prepared for his wonder."

Isn't that beautiful?

Thomas Merton, in a letter to a friend, reveals his way of experiencing such prayer:

"Strictly speaking, the very simple way of prayer is centered entirely on attention to the presence of God and to his will and to his love. That is to say that it is centered on faith by which alone we can know the presence of God. My prayer is then a kind of praise rising up out of

the centre of nothingness and silence. If I'm still present myself, this I recognize as an obstacle. If he wills he can then make the nothingness into total clarity."

Grace Brame, in her work *Receptive Prayer* offers a clear expression of the practice and purpose of prayer. She defines this Receptive Prayer as a means of becoming *in tune with the infinite.* She further defines this tuning and binding as coming through *a relaxation of the body in God's presence.* Surely we know that we can't approach God while we're disturbed and tight with tension. We must come into a state of relaxation, of letting go, with a dedication of the will to God and a commitment, or a focusing of the mind on God with an open receptivity to the spirit of God.

Appealing to our scientific view of reality, the author also observes that our state of mind can, and does, stimulate the pituitary gland which, through the production of hormones, directs and affects the whole body. This process causes the flow of endorphins, which are protein substances manufactured in the body that are natural pain killers, and known to produce feelings of *well being.* So when you pray in this way, your body actually manufactures these natural pain killers. How about that for a side effect? If you take the fake kind of pain killers, you get another kind of side effect, don't you?

More importantly, the attitude created and reinforced by receptive prayer is one of being positive, hopeful, trusting and expectant. Brame states that receptive prayer is a holistic way of praying, the results of which are far beyond superstition or mechanical prayer. She says the one who prays, accepts the responsibility of *being part of the answering process,* of even finding the answer in the almost wholly undiscovered world within himself. This sort of prayer is not a coaxing of the divine, but rather, a receiving of what God already has in store for us.

This receptivity allows us to be instructed and to accept the reality of grace and its transforming power. She says that after relaxing the body and focusing the mind, the next absolutely essential step in the prayer of commitment to God is a form of directed yielding to God's creative change. A period of soaking in. Soaking in follows when we're receptive to the love and peace and presence surrounding us. Just soaking it in. Not asking God anything, not wanting anything, but just being with the spirit.

Then, other gifts may be received. It may be guidance for a problem posed, or understanding of a person who is either loved or disliked. Here, we intercede for others by sharing in spirit with them or by being taught to understand their needs. We have *centered in order to expand outwards.* Receptive Prayer is *not* selfish. In giving ourselves to God, we are more able to give ourselves to others. This way of praying is a pathway of revelation. To this form of prayer we both receive and transmit information, energy and emotion. We become a channel for God's grace and expression of incarnate love. It is God who does the work, but he's not just out there somewhere, he is in and through his creation.

The highest use of Receptive Prayer is to allow God to permeate our being. This form of Christian meditation is different from secular or manipulative uses of meditation adapted for positive thinking, relaxation, or concentration. The goal here is an openness to God, centered commitment and contact, and a willingness to rest upon, release, and yield to God so that we can be more completely his, enabling his creating to continue in us and his creativity to flow through us. We become co-creators with God.

We are told that if we faithfully persevere, every obstacle will gradually be removed and inward silence will become easier. It is primarily due to a lack of this inward recollection that we are so rarely aware of the divine light. It should therefore become our daily practice, because the less we practice silent prayer, *the less we desire it.* If you've never done it, you don't know what you're missing. You don't realize what it can do for you.

Writer and retreat leader father Basil Pennington suggests three rules that synthesize and simplify hundreds of years of wisdom on the practice of prayer:

Rule 1: At the beginning of prayer take a minute or two to quiet down and then move in faith to God dwelling in our depths. And at the end of the prayer take several minutes to come out of our inner sanctuary.

Rule 2: After resting for a time in the centre of our being, take up a single simple word or two that expresses your response to this encounter and begin to let it repeat itself within. Some examples, perhaps, are: *thank you; forgive me; amen; Lord Jesus;* or *have mercy.*

Rule 3: Whenever in the course of the prayer we become aware of anything else, we simply return to the prayer word.

Thomas Kelly names the depth of prayer *inward listening*, and comments: "Prayer is a two way process. It's not just human souls whispering to God. It passes over into communion with God active in us as well as we active toward God. A specific state of expectancy, of openness of soul is laid bare and receptive before the eternal goodness. In quietness, we wait."

Merton insists that we need not strain or strive after spiritual encounter through prayer, as the spirit is already with us. It is simply a matter of giving it a chance to make itself known to us.

Spiritual directors of all ages have offered three basic counsels to persons seeking God through prayer:

1) Do not wait until you feel like praying, or you will stop praying when you need it most.

2) To desire to pray is already a result of prayer.

3) Know that God is waiting for you.

And this is a fourth one: Never forget that the less you pray, the more poorly you do it, and the less you will desire it. Imagine going farther and farther away and adrift from your centre, from your source, from God. There are terrible consequences when we simply don't pay attention to prayer.

Douglas Steel speaks of the loss of oneself which suddenly leads one into a deeper and faster encounter with reality. This is a wonderful passage that I've always loved:

"How good to remember how in prayer one day my tight detailed petitions were all blown aside as though they were dandelion fluff. How I stopped praying and began to be prayed in, how I died and was literally melted down by the love of a power that coursed through my heart sweeping away the hard claim for core and poured through me a torrent of infinite tenderness and caring."

May you know that experience someday.

There are certain basic elements that must be present in the preparation of turning to God. We all need quiet and solitude for the practice of prayer. This is not to say that a quiet mind cannot be found in the midst of a crowd, but such a capacity to seal oneself from the distractions of the senses is a gift and a discipline that is rarely achieved. We must begin with God, not with ourselves, when we pray.

Brother Lawrence speaks to us of practicing the presence of God. This simply means to live constantly in God's presence and to know that we are living in his presence. He took seriously the words of Jesus in Matthew 28:20, *I am with you always.*

Love is the key to practicing or experiencing the presence of God. Our relationship with God is one of love. Because we love him, we are eager to be in his presence. So the love of God becomes the purpose and goal of all our actions. When we know that God is with us all the time, we live for him alone. We place ourselves entirely in his hands that he may do with us and through us what he wills. This practice is certainly not easy, it requires every ounce of will power and effort and self sacrifice of which we are capable. Yet we cannot tell anyone how to live in the presence of God. We can only point out that we begin by *becoming receptive* to spiritual presence and *accepting the movements of grace.* Our work is *to never give up* and to always begin again.

In a Christian context, because we live and move and have our being in God, being present to things as they are involves encountering the Christ, who, according to Ephesians 1:23, fills the whole creation. In other words, Christian contemplation means finding God in all things and all things in God. Brother Lawrence called it *the loving gaze which finds God everywhere.*

In this sense, contemplation is an all embracing quality of presence, included not only in our inner experience, but also directly perceiving and responding to the needs of the world around us. Rather than trying to balance contemplation and action, it's more accurate to see *contemplation in action* undergirding and embracing everything. In this way, knowing, acting, and feeling can all be joined together in prayerful openness and loving responsiveness.

Most of us have been taught to concentrate, to focus attention on one thing at a time. The contemplative traditions, however, maintain that we function more lovingly, and can be more in touch with our desire for God's guidance when we are more widely open to what is going on. So many of the contemplatively oriented practices involve *an unlearning* of our habit of focusing attention. In its place, one hopes to nurture a simple willingness to be open to God's movements, leadings and invitations.

You can see how focused attention would give you tunnel vision, where not even God can get through. Hyper focus and part of the relaxing and surrendering, just sort of opens your peripheral awareness of everything around you. Actual contemplation happens only when God takes over and carries us beyond ourselves – beyond where we either could or would choose to go on our own. The gift comes when and how God desires to give it, and lasts for as long as God chooses. Moreover, it usually takes place in obscurity, without the person comprehending what is happening. John of the Cross said contemplation occurs in the *notte obscura,* the dark night of the soul. In this hidden process, God increasingly frees the person for love. It's amazing how suffering can free you of yourself. It is the gift of love that gives contemplation its meaning and its direction towards the fulfillment of the two great commandments.

When we undertake new efforts like these suggested for deep prayer, we expect to get something out of these enterprises, and we are likely to become impatient with ourselves if the results aren't forthcoming. If we feel we're not making sufficient progress, we tend to look for results, whether in the form of insight, peace of mind, healing, or some other substantial benefit. But a contemplative perspective maintains that although such things may happen, they are by no means the goal of the spiritual life. In fact whether they happen or not is almost irrelevant. *The spiritual life is about love, not about particular accomplishments.* Further contemplative view honors a sense of mystery and unknowing, and it encourages dependence upon God's grace and mercy to guide and carry us where God would have us go.

The first and most important way of exploring your spiritual life is to sincerely attend to your own prayer. Take sufficient quiet time to pray for God's grace and guidance, for understanding, for a sense of direction, for clarity about your desire for God and God's desire for you. Listen carefully, waiting openly for a sense of rightness about next steps. Let yourself be guided toward the disciplines, practices and resources that are called for in your life now.

This process of transformation is the goal of the spiritual life. The aim of methods of prayer is to allow those conditions to immerge in which divine light may shine clearly and without interruption – conditions in which the soul is led to clear vision of God. The path to the depth of prayer involves both self-discovery and self-surrender. The devotional lives of the men and women quoted here reveal to us the most direct way to an attainment of the consciousness of our spiritual environment, which the mystics call *the presence of God.*

It is our birthright to achieve a simple kind of contemplation that opens on to such life-giving awareness, but after all the wisdom has been learned and the techniques tested, we must remember the conclusion of a mystic of the seventeenth century. He said the *greatest method in prayer is to have none.* This paradox was resolved by the profound observation of Saint Augustine, one of the greatest teachers at the Western church. In his words: *We come to God by love and not by navigation.*

The contemplative journey is an adventure in faith, a trip into the unknown. If we think we know what is going to happen, or if we expect to arrive at certain goals, we're on the wrong road. The moment you surrender yourself to God, you're surrendering to an unknown future and destiny. You're letting yourself become the person whom God always intended you to be. We learn through the spirit's guidance, through difficult and impossible situations, to relinquish our hold on every level of our being, allowing God to take total possession so that we can manifest the pure love of God in daily life without even thinking about it.

The noise and frenetic character of modern life, the excessive chatter, so much information, so much entertainment, all of this has to quiet down inside of us. The greatest teacher is silence. To come out of interior silence and to practice its radiance, its love, its concern for others, its submission to God's will, its trust in God even in tragic situations, is the fruit of living from our inmost centre, from the contemplative space within. The signs that come from this space are a peace that is rarely upset by events or by other people and our reactions to them, and a calm that is a stabilizing force in whatever environment you may be in. Imagine being a stabilizing force everywhere you go. God can use people like that.

God gives us everything we need to be happy in the present moment, no matter what evidence there is to the contrary. Now that's faith. Our prayer as contemplative persons is the constant exercise of faith, hope and love. It takes place in the silence of our hearts as we listen to the word of God, not just with our ears or minds, but with our inmost being. God speaks best by silence. This does not mean that we do not have unwanted thoughts in prayer, but that we return again and again to the basic consent of self surrender and trust. We say yes to that presence and every now and then we enter into union with it as we identify the divine presence in Christ's humanity with the divine presence within us.

When we say *Come Lord Jesus, Maranatha*, we should remember that Christ is already here and that his coming simply means that he becomes more and more present to our consciousness. He does not move, we move. This process begins first with consent to God's presence, then surrender, and finally transformation into it. As we learn to listen to the word of God within us, we develop greater sensitivity to the gifts of the spirit, allowing the divine energy to manifest itself during prayer and in the events of daily life. And this enables us to lead our human life in a divine way.

Be still and know that I am God.

2

Meister Eckhart and the Birth Within

"He spoke to you from the point of view of eternity, but you understood him from the point of view of time."

- John Tauler, Student of Meister Eckhart

Meister Eckhart lived between 1260 and 1327. He was a Dominican scholar, a popular preacher, and a teacher in Paris, Strasbourg and Cologne. Today, he is one of the most powerful influences on the cutting edge of Christian mysticism and a key link between Eastern and Western insights into the evolution of human consciousness. The Church excommunicated this German Master even though he claimed to be its loyal son to the end of his days. But his experience of God soared so high that it transcended the need for priests and sacraments. Everything he wrote concerning the encounter with the Divine was based on immediate, personal experience, which is why he is as vital a guide at the end of the twentieth century as he was at the beginning of the fourteenth.

In 1980, at the General Chapter of Walberberg, representatives of the Order of Preachers gathered to consider the Papal bull of 1329 which condemned as heretical fifteen articles or statements expressed by Meister Eckhart. At issue was their concern that a terrible injustice had been done to the great teacher. For those who are familiar with the luminous mystic's words, it is no surprise that the dogmatically-bound bishops of the Church were shocked, even scandalized by his teachings. The following was condemned in Article 8 of the bull, known as *In Agro*

Dominico: "Those who are not desiring possessions, or honors, or gain, or internal devotion, or holiness, or reward or the kingdom of heaven, but who have renounced all this, even what is theirs, these people pay honor to God."

The times in which he spoke such radical and original words were very much like our own. A great spiritual upheaval was taking place. There was a movement called "Liberty of Spirit," ancestor to our New Age approach to awakening; there was a new "enlightenment" brought by the discovery of Arabic, Hebrew and Greek thought which was causing people to found their beliefs on reason rather than on the heart; at the same time, universities were packed with pedantic, hair-splitting academics utterly insulated from the life-giving depths of the Faith; the Church itself had lost prestige as the Pope's authority was called into question, and the selling of indulgences made grotesquely clear the financial lusts of the institution. Finally, a great many lay movements were arising in reaction to the sterile teachings of Rome. Men and women who were seeking the living waters of spiritual consciousness came together to create loosely connected groups such as "the Friends of God" and magnificent works like "The Imitation of Christ," "Theologia Germanica," and Mechtild of Magdeburg's "The Light of the Godhead."

The visionaries born from the religious turmoil of the fourteenth century, Jacob Boheme, John Ruysbroeck, and Julian of Norwich, were all influenced by the mighty spiritual light of Meister Eckhart, whose legacy includes spiritual treatises such as the *Book of Divine Consolation*, the *Talks on Instruction* and *On Detachment*, along with his eighty-six sermons, each of which is a window into the inexpressible. The flight of his thought was so lofty that in modern times, parallels have been drawn between his insights and those of Zen Buddhism. Even a cursory review of Eckhart's sermons and writings will reveal this unique connection. He says of the Godhead for example: *"He is He because He is not He. This contradiction can be comprehended by the inner man, and not by the outer man."* Eckhart is referring here to his view that at the heart of God's "identity" is the fact that He must go out of Himself. This is the very essence of Love, and students of Neoplatonism will also recognize in this concept Plato's idea of the "overflow of the One."

In considering the reasons for his condemnation, it is essential to understand that Meister Eckhart spoke to a variety of audiences, and most especially to the Dominican nuns who were highly educated and deeply mystically inclined. It is true that the "sublime teacher" spoke words and used images which were often difficult to grasp by those unfamiliar with the inner experience he was attempting to describe. His treatise *On John's Gospel* is generally considered his most mature work. He also left behind an unfinished outline for what would have been the culmination of his life's work. This massive undertaking which he had called the *Opus Tripartitum*, the "Three-Part Work," was to organize and clarify his mystical theology and might have possibly convinced his detractors that he was indeed a "loyal son of the Church." It has been recorded that, on his deathbed, he did reject any of his statements which might have seemed heretical, but this is misleading. As he stepped into eternity, the old master was steadfast in holding to his extraordinary views. He was, above all, a lover of God.

Eckhart had an extraordinarily modern understanding of the nature of being and of human psychology. He saw us as fragmented and separated from our source of origin with an "irrepressible orientation" toward our spiritual unity. But he provided no dogma as signposts on the way. He considered it better to say what God is not rather than what God is. He believed that each had to find his or her own path to the Godhead within, and that this search could take place anywhere. In simplest terms, he believed that God is immediately present to us and that through the abandonment of our lower selves and their world of multiplicity, we can be filled with the eternal illumination of the unmediated, inexpressible Godhead. In one of his best known sermons, "The Kingdom of God is at Hand," Meister Eckhart states that "man's blessedness depends on his awareness and recognition of the highest good: God Himself." This fundamental thesis of Eckhart's thought reveals a number of underlying presuppositions. The term "highest good" is taken directly from Neoplatonic mysticism inherited from Plotinus, Augustine, and the Pseudo-Dionysius. We can infer from this appropriation that Eckhart uses another major Platonic idea – the theme of the soul's return to the One.

He hints at this view of reality when he states that God "expects the soul to progress to that point where it may receive much." Progress is therefore equated with knowing, a knowing which is not based on empirical observation or rational comprehension, but rather on an inner, higher level of consciousness which transcends the material world. Meister Eckhart considers the intellect as the element in us which opens onto higher spiritual spheres. This perception makes of it far more than the workings of the reasoning mind. The intellect is the "agent" within the soul which is "perfectly sensitive to God" because it is of God's order and not made from nature. Awareness of reality comes through the development or transformation of this agent "into God." The consciousness of the nearness of God reveals for Eckhart that all reality depends on the invisible and immanent reality of the Divine: "my being depends on God's intimate presence."

The material, historical dimension of reality is seen as the lowest level from which the soul must become detached. This most important idea of detachment assumes that time and space are "fragments" and that unity (the highest good and truth) is found only in God. As heaven is therefore outside of time and space, so the soul must be "equidistant from every earthly thing." The soul's knowledge of God is hindered by time and space because their multiplicity veils the unity from which everything comes. "If I am to know true being, I must know it where it is being itself, and that is in God and not where it is divided among creatures." Knowing God outside of time and space means knowing God in His fullness, His purity.

For Eckhart, this is the Kingdom of God, the state of being in which all creation is known in its essence, the origin and home of the soul. The ascent of the soul to the Kingdom of God is an inward journey: "God is within; we are without." The outer physical realm can only distract the soul in a way that is best expressed by Augustine's two loves, i.e., the mistaken preference of love of the creation over love of the Creator.

Eckhart asserts that if sticks and stones knew God in His immanent presence, they would be "as blessed as the angels." He suggests that the only true difference between a stick and a human being is precisely in this matter of knowing God's nearness. This consciousness is not a matter of instruction but of inner experience or "recognition." "When the Kingdom appears to the soul and it is recognized, there is no further need for preaching or instruction." This capacity to live in the Kingdom now, or outside of time while still in time, is possible for humanity. The key is the annihilation of the will with its blindness and misconceptions through detachment and surrender. Such a life is only possible through a stripping away of all differences between the center of the inner man and its source, the Godhead. "You must be empty so that you may be filled." This is not some outdated asceticism, but the peeling away of all that is artificial in us and keeps us from true wholeness and fulfillment.

Eckhart reveals here the danger of mysticism for the Church as an institution and power structure in the world, when he insists that God is "equally near" to everything and every place, and that a person knows Him only when they know how to see Him under all circumstances. "To sit in church and recognize Him" is due to man's defective nature. Eckhart's mysticism is radically immanent and centered on an unmediated relationship to reality. Detachment from temporality requires that the soul be "so firm and steady in God that nothing can penetrate it," an idea found in the Stoics as well as in other mystics. This renunciation of the material world does not come from a Gnostic concept of evil inherent in matter, but from a view of true being as outside of time and infinitely superior and removed from corporeal things and the illusions arising out of this fragment of reality. Nothing from without must penetrate the spiritually ascending soul, including itself.

The consciousness of God excludes the consciousness of oneself until one finds oneself again in God. Here Eckhart is suggesting a merger with the divine where no medium separates the soul from the Godhead. The intellect must have no existence of its own in order to be filled with the only true existence.

This union is accomplished in the moment when the receptive intellect is transformed into God's fullness. Becoming one with the spirit of God is the way to unity, rest, and true freedom. For Eckhart, God is always near to us and we are far from him to the extent that we are lost in the passions, in the senses, and in the fragmentation which we take to be ourselves. The transformations which Christians undergo recreate them into the indistinct Oneness of the Creator. Grace conforms them to Christ in a way that leaves no separation between the Word and the creature. The dwelling among us of the Word made flesh is the entrance of the uncreated into the emptied created, of eternity into time. Eckhart avoids what Church dogma would consider heresy by distinguishing between the Only-Begotten, the "natural" Son of God, and those begotten from a rebirth that leads to conformity with this divine nature. The difference makes us "sons" by adoption, though Eckhart insists that our natures are fused with the divine nature.

He further clarifies this point by stating that Christ is the Father's image, whereas we are made in the image of the Trinity. In other words, Christ is the likeness of the hidden Godhead, while we are the likeness of the first emanation. There is no trace here of a univocal identification between the witnesses and the witnessed. Eckhart underscores the continuity between nature and the Eternal. The properties of the things of nature do in fact teach that which is found in the Holy Scriptures. As the soul is united to the flesh in order to form a human being, so too does the Word dwell in every work of nature. The same act of existence, the Father's begetting, is found in all that lives.

This oneness suggests an integration between body and soul which leaves no separation within the hierarchy of being. Eckhart carries this Aristotelian principle into Plato's pre-existent ideas about creation: The artist's idea of his particular piece of work constitutes the full existence of that yet unnamed object. Therefore, as an iron bar heated by fire becomes at least as hot as the fire, so does the soul born from the Spirit become capable of performing works of the Spirit.

This insight assumes an absorption of the lower into the higher in which the lower is utterly consumed. The lower actually becomes the higher. When the Word made flesh dwells within us, we become directly present to the glory of the Unbegotten; we see His glory, and therefore we are His glory. This is how Eckhart understands the fullness of our joy. As with wood and fire, we too can enter into a higher form and "glow" with the very glow of holiness itself. This is the birth of the Son in the soul, the unmediated first emanation of the Godhead in an individual. Eckhart takes the Neoplatonic return theme and carries it beyond rest in God or vision of God, into an actual oneness in which there is no distinction whatsoever. He presupposes that everything is divine in its ground, that the soul has a spark of uncreated light at its core, and that the total emptying or abandonment of the self results in the soul's penetration into the naked Godhead Itself, the source of all being.

Multiplicity, restlessness, changeability cease only when there is no more becoming. As with the pain of physical birth, there is initially a "painful unlikeness that resists change."

When birth takes place, or when the wood has received the form of fire, the generation raises the lower substance into the begetting realm which transcends time and creation. The birth within, which forms Christ in the soul, makes us "sons of God" because "every unlikeness has been cast off." Then we are no longer troubled by many things, like Martha the sister of Lazarus, but we will have chosen, like Mary her contemplative sister, the best part which will not be taken away from us. This choice, which is actually a receptivity created by detachment and humility, allows us to ask "in the Son's name," which is a state of experiencing the divine in an inward silence where there is nothing more to ask.

To achieve such a mystical union, Eckhart has assumed that God is the author of all truth, wherever that truth may be found. He assumes that all statements on truth can be harmonized into one which is available to reason.

Spiritual truths therefore do not transcend the powers of reason. Reason is then for Eckhart that which constitutes the image of God. Even the divine mysteries can be penetrated by reason. More importantly perhaps is the Meister's assertion that the soul and God share the same ground. Everything in its essence is divine. The "divine darkness" of the hidden Godhead, source of all things, has now become accessible. This becomes understandable if one considers Eckhart's presupposition that only the highest reality is the truly real. In the illustration of the wood and the fire, the wood's becoming fire is possible because the fire is more real than the wood. Since human existence is only a partial existence, the implication is that it can flow back into absolute existence. As with cause and effect, we are pre-contained in that which supremely Is. Since multiplicity is evil, or lower and therefore a defect, the Christian's task is to leave this realm through a monastic-like humility which completely rejects the will of the small self and searches out the one Desire behind all desire.

To achieve union with God, which is actually to receive God, there can be no medium between the soul and the Godhead. The intellect therefore must have no existence of its own in order to be filled with the only true existence. Meister Eckhart believes that when this emptying is achieved, the soul is lifted up to God and established in an eternal turning away from all sin. God's presence then shines through this emptiness and reveals Him in all that the Christian sees and does. "You ought to sink down out of all your your-ness, and flow into his his-ness, and your 'yours' and his 'his' ought to become one 'mine,' so completely that you with him perceive forever his uncreated is-ness, and his nothingness, for which there is no name."

3

Watchfulness

Rediscovering an Ancient Tradition from Early Christianity

One of the keys to opening the door leading to our true nature is found in the most common element of our psyche: attention. Early Christian teachers recognized it as central to spiritual development. An elementary definition of attention might be that it is a focusing of our energy onto a subject of interest. We all know instinctively when this inner power waxes and wanes. We can remember from school days how often we found our attention wandering off into realms of fantasy or to the scenery outside the window. With maturity, we may have found it necessary to develop that "muscle" of concentration to keep ourselves engaged in a particular task.

What many people have not realized is that this same intangible power of attention is critical to our spiritual awakening. If we let it dissipate into the countless distractions of life, we will find that our life force is drained, unavailable for our ultimate task of conscious existence. Most of us lack the self-awareness that is required to realize the dignity of being human. From the character driving down the highway more focused on his daydreams than on the road and the lives of those around him, to the thoughtless parent who shames his child, this lack of inner attention is the cause of our continual stumbling. Self-awareness and the subsequent discovery of the divine are rare in human behavior because they require energy.

We squander most of the "psychic gold" of our attention on things from fidgeting to outbursts of anger. It can wipe out a whole day's ration of energy, as can constant talking, daydreaming, worrying, and other energy "leaks." Watchfulness requires that we pay attention to the thoughts, impulses and desires vying for expression and satisfaction. This attention itself may prevent them from taking control. Through this effort we acquire self-mastery and establish a stable foundation for our inner transformation.

Nothing can be accomplished if we are not dependable or mindful of our commitment. We cannot be of use to ourselves or to anyone else if we are constantly tossed about by the waves of our inner chaos. We gain a "clear sight" when we lift ourselves above the thoughts and feelings that struggle with each other within us. This is not merely a psychological trick, but clears the ground and makes room to receive the inflow of a higher power.

Spiritual teachers throughout the Christian Tradition tell us that learning how not to respond to external stimulus is a necessary step for inner development. The effect of not reacting to an external event does not imply a cold, disconnected relationship to life. Detachment, as understood in the classical mystical tradition, is not removal from life, but from one's own uncontrolled emotions and attitudes.

The teachings gathered in the "Philokalia" from the great spiritual masters of early Christianity, offer specific ways of developing these inner powers. Turned inwardly, attention stands guard over images coming in from without and thoughts arising from within. Persistent awareness insures that both stimuli are kept from further influencing our behavior. For once the image is allowed to penetrate within, it is on the way to being materialized into action.

Thus protected, the heart is by nature capable of giving birth from within itself to thoughts of a more conscious nature. External reality now comes to us without our filters of expectations, prejudices, and judgments that otherwise mar our view. The experts in inner warfare tell us that we should wage this war with a focused and united will that disperses fantasies. The intellect then no longer pursues them "like a child deceived by some conjurer" (Philokalia, saying 105). The masters further claim that such watchfulness gives us knowledge, enlightenment, and instruction previously unattainable by our intellect while we were still "walking in the murk of passions and dark deeds, in forgetfulness and in the confusion of chaos" (saying 116).

Such watchfulness leads to the creation of an "inner sanctuary" which is the point where God and the soul touch. In the fourteenth century, John Tauler, a student of Meister Eckhart, referred to this place as "the ground of the soul." Catherine of Siena spoke of the "interior home of the heart," Teresa of Ávila knew it as the "inner castle," and John of the Cross described it as the "house at rest in darkness and concealment." These metaphors suggest a secret dwelling in the center of our being that remains permanently united with God's creative act. The self in its deepest nature is more than itself. To move into oneself means ultimately to move beyond oneself.

The Way of Inner Silence

Few western people know that the idea of "inner silence" is at the heart of the earliest expressions of Christian practice and faith. This way of being has a name that has yet to be uncovered in our part of the world. The Greek word "hesychia" has been a fundamental spiritual practice in the traditions of Eastern Orthodox Christianity going back to the first centuries after the appearance of the Anointed One in the hill country of Judea. This mysterious word can be translated as "inner tranquility" or "inner silence" and a complex psychological teaching and set of practices has grown up around it, involving some of the great figures of eastern Christianity such as Saint Gregory Palamas, John Cassian, and many others. Hesychasm is a quality of conscious presence that combines constant inner awareness and prayer with deep stillness. It requires a profound self-knowledge, attentiveness to each breath of the body, and commitment to the reality of the sacred at the heart of life. A synthesis of this teaching can be found in a revered book known as "The Philokalia" (translated as "Love of Beauty" or "Love of the Good") which is central to Orthodox spirituality.

The teaching on "*hesychia*" is modeled in many ways by the actions of Jesus as recorded in the Gospels, but especially in the strange scene presented in Luke 4:28-33, after Jesus had revealed his mission to the people of his hometown: "All the people in the synagogue were furious when they heard this. They got up, drove him out of the town, and took him to the brow of the hill on which the town was built, in order to throw him down the cliff. But he walked right through the crowd and went on his way."

In the midst of violent attack, he maintained an attitude of extraordinary inner peace – as he would later on the way to the cross – and responded to the hatred and fury with silence and a detachment that mystically saved him from harm.

Though particularly evident in the humility and inner grounding of the Christ, "hesychasm" is a universal concept. Its parallel can be found in other ideas related to spiritual evolution, such as detachment, freedom from desire and inner peace. The results of this effort are seen in the presence of sages and saints in all times and places.

Inner silence ultimately means self-transcendence. It requires us to overcome a fundamental self-interest that guides everyone's life in order to accept the difficulties of passing circumstances, and to remember the greater context in which our lives are taking place. Accomplishing the inner freedom which leads to inner silence is no passive effort. In fact, it demands "inner warfare" as we seek to become liberated from all that is connected with the inherent selfishness in which we are born, including the self-absorption of relentless thoughts, most of them based on self-interest. This condition is part of our natural make-up, as basic to us as the instinct to survive. The paradox we all must face is that spiritual and psychological survival requires the opposite of this natural instinct. The maturing of the human character means turning one's attention to something greater than oneself, which then offers a basis for inner stability, independence from externals, and a peace that "passes all understanding."

To be without this inner silence founded on the spiritual consciousness of a greater reality is to literally lose ourselves in the stimuli of the outside world and in the hallucinations of our imaginations, fears, daydreams and vacuous illusions.

The serenity that is witnessed in the sages and saints of the past is not meant to be some rare or unique nobility of character. It is right alignment with reality, an achievable state for all of us and no less than our birthright, if we are willing to struggle for it.

This inner freedom has nothing to do with emotional disconnection, lack of compassion or disinterest in what is going on around us. In fact, to be rooted in an active state of inner silence gives one the widest scope of vision and makes possible a new awareness and a capacity for unconditional love.

This is very difficult work, as anyone will quickly discover upon making efforts to overcome the noise of our relentless and random thoughts and feelings. It demands moment by moment remembrance of our true purpose in this world, and a constant check on our automatic reactions based on acquired habits and imitations of those around us. The "hesychastic" way calls us to take the state of calm found in deep meditation and carry it with us into the noise and tumult of daily life.

To follow this way of inner silence requires the capacity to accept necessary suffering, a fact that everyone must deal with in one way or another. To experience inner pain without falling victim to self-pity or despair is a sign of a new maturity of will and understanding. At the apex of this way of being is the ability to find joy and gratitude for the gift of life even in the face of great turmoil, injustice, or tragedy. Living in that paradox creates a new quality of Self which transcends the ever-shifting scenery of temporal life. This inner silence is the groundwork of unity, constancy and true freedom.

4

The Dark Night of the Soul

Have you ever felt empty and abandoned, not just by people, but by God? Unable to feel the way you once felt, unable to experience joy, unable to pray? These are symptoms of a condition called by centuries of spiritual teachers "the dark night of the soul." Those of you who know these symptoms only too well ought to take heart at the mere fact that this condition is not unique to your situation. This "night" is a specific stage along the path of spiritual development. Not only are you not alone in this experience, but it is quite possibly a sign that you are moving forward in the direction toward which your heart is yearning.

One of the great teachers on this subject is the Spanish mystic, poet and monk, John of the Cross (1542-1591). He wrote some of the most beautiful poetry ever penned in the Spanish language and then authored entire books as commentaries on each stanza.

John of the Cross said the following about the dark night: "Even though this blessed night darkens the spirit, it does so only to impart light in all things. And even though it humbles us and reveals our miseries, it does so only to exalt us. And even though it impoverishes us and empties us of all our possessions and natural affections, it does so only that we may reach forward divinely to the enjoyment of everything in heaven and on earth, all the while preserving a general freedom of spirit in them all."

As in all spiritual insights, these ideas require the reconciliation of opposites in order to be understood. According to the mystical tradition, the darkness which is so oppressive to us can turn out to be light itself. The desolation of the soul becomes a purification from selfishness and desires in order to clear the ground for the reception of greater wisdom and joy. It can develop a new ability to perceive and understand: through unknowing we come to truly know. These paradoxes are much more than mind-bending sayings. They represent the essence of the human experience of divine reality. We can never hope to know the creative force of the universe with our tiny minds, nor can we understand the depth and breadth of the purpose of life in its objective totality. This is why faith is at the center of spiritual teachings. Not faith as adherence to a belief system which is passively accepted, but faith as a powerful, courageous opening of the heart and mind beyond the realm of the senses.

It should be no big secret to thinking persons that life cannot simply be taken at face value. If the sum total of existence is fully explained on the six o'clock newscast, then we confine ourselves to a narrow and essentially meaningless view of why we are here. Most of what we see on the surface of life is little more than chaos. Yet something within us senses that there is a greater mystery behind it all. Fine art and music, or a glorious sunset can often strike a chord that carries us beyond the mundane insanity of daily life. The same can be said for our suffering and sadness. Those of us who have cried out in prayer for help or who are plagued with desperate loneliness must open themselves to the possibility that they are being heard and answered, but not as they expect.

To journey with perseverance through the seeming endlessness of such dark times will lead to another shore. The very acceptance of these unacceptable times is part of the answer. Maturity of character, release from self-absorption and new depths of courage eventually give birth to another self. This is a self that understands in ways that the mind cannot grasp, that has gone out of itself in order to find itself, and that sees what other eyes cannot see. This is the self that comes from the deep running river of the soul, no longer from the surface persona we know so well.

We have to face the fact that life is not meant to be a banquet of satisfactions for our particular interests. We are here for a much nobler purpose, one that links us with creation as a whole. It is the sense of being isolated entities that causes a great deal of our dysfunction and sorrow. As we claim our true worth as children of the universe, we recognize the self-sacrificial aspect of our purpose here.

We are not on this earth merely to gratify ourselves or to have every passing wish come true. We are here as beings endowed with higher consciousness and willpower for the very specific aim of being useful to the purposes of our Creator. Just as a parent has the absolute obligation to care for his or her child, so must we care for the beings (human, animal, vegetable) placed upon our path and, in so doing, spread harmony and healing to the world around us. If we do not, if we plant ourselves squarely on our own acre of self-interest, then our days upon this planet will have been wasted.

However, in order to be able to become participants in the care of the world, we must maintain our link with our ineffable Maker. This we cannot do as long as our selfishness, self-gratification, and ignorance stand in the way. We must be empty in order to be filled, say the mystics. Filled with what? The awareness of the holiness of life. The preliminary emptying is the dark night of the soul. When our reason can no longer make sense of what is taking place, when we have to surrender ourselves into invisible arms that don't seem to be there, then we become empowered with a consciousness of deeper reality that nothing can ever take away from us.

Spirituality has been described as the degree to which we are in touch with reality and the dark night is the process of going ever further through those degrees. It is true that many people suffer from despair that leads nowhere and that has no transforming value. Such sorrow leads only to bleakness and an emptiness that is not fertile with the Presence of God. In this case, a person must pray for and find those who can help them turn this grief into new understanding.

The fact is that every human experience can be fuel for wisdom and if there is any message that religions and metaphysics have taught us down through the centuries, it is that there is always cause for hope! Someday we will each be able to say: "Death, where is thy victory?"

Then we will see from a new perspective all the sufferings that caused us such anxiety and hopelessness. The dark night of the soul teaches us to know through unknowing, to see in the darkness, to find meaning in meaninglessness, and union in solitude. It is the mystery of mysteries, the deepest secret of all religions, and the very core of what it means to be human.

To accept our pain, our mortality, and say "yes" to life, opens onto a transcendence that frees us from it all. The dark night refers to the times when it seems that we are down for the count, when nothing can lift us up, when there is no help, no hope and no way out. Yet the mystics of all ages make it very clear that this is precisely when we are asked to hope more than ever. This is precisely when we are being worked with most closely.

We must get beyond our senses and our natural inclinations if we wish to enter the supernatural dimensions of spiritual awareness. Sometimes this requires that all the lights be turned out, that we walk alone in the dark, in the night of uncertainty and confusion. A friend once told me that it was when circumstances had shattered him that he truly encountered the reality of God. In his despair and brokenness, he nevertheless felt himself mysteriously held up by a compassionate force. Having gone to the heart of hopelessness, he found there an inexpressible Presence that came to his aid and kept him going.

Since then, that Presence has made itself known to him in more vivid ways. According to the classic spiritual tradition represented by John of the Cross, "the purifying and loving divine light operates within us as does fire upon wood which transforms the wood into itself." The idea expressed here is that acceptance of spiritual suffering results in a spiritual activity that leads to transforming union with the Source of our being. John of the Cross tells us: "In order to arrive at being everything, desire to be nothing."

These are difficult teachings indeed and demand great strength of character. But so does living rightly on this planet. If we choose to be more than a slave to our every impulse and seek the dignity of being a child of the universe capable of witnessing the wonder of life and of participating in its care-taking, then we need to be grounded in something other than our own desires and satisfactions.

This is where the dark night can be useful to us: it can create new foundations made out of patience, perseverance, and a faith in the ultimate goodness of the universe which nothing will be able to destroy. Certainly it means sacrifice and acceptance of pain and insecurity. But this is what creates a spiritual being who can care for the unlovely and put up with the twists and turns of existence until the time when it enters into an even greater darkness which, some say, turns out to be the most wondrous light of all.

5

Dante's Mystical Journey

Medieval understanding of sin as perceived by a brilliant writer such as Dante, presents us with a potency of spiritual awareness which puts our age to shame. His efforts were aimed at revealing the magnitude of our blasphemy as we live out our indulgent, empty lives in the presence of the spiritual universe which silently watches our tragic self-idolatry. The brooding poet exhibited extraordinary insight into psychology, a fact which ought to cleanse our modern minds from any sense of superiority over his use of imagery, however steeped it might have been in the gruesome dramatics of the "Dark Ages." Dante stands in the company of the prophets of the Old Testament when he denounces the darkness of the human soul. His deserts and lakes of boiling pitch are the hell of the putrid inner life in which much of humankind finds itself.

O you proud Christians, wretched souls and small, who by the dim lights of your twisted minds believe you prosper even as you fall. (Purg. c.16, 91-93)

One does not crawl out of "Beelzebub's dim tomb," where Dante dreaded death as never before, where the winds of Cocytus exhale evil and its punishment from the whirling wings of the Emperor of the Universe of Pain, without discovering that this fourteenth century manuscript has pierced its way into that private realm where the soul must face itself.

Dante meets us at a place many people have come to know. "How I came to it I cannot rightly say, so drugged and loose with sleep had I become, when I first wandered from the True Way." Within the multi-dimensional meanings of The Divine Comedy lies Dante's own struggle with himself, with outer life, and with the awakening of spiritual perception. The poet leads us to the grim shore where "all must come who lose the fear of God." There he proclaims that sinners "yearn for what they fear." The heart of the sinner is deliberately hardened to the love of the Creator, for divine grace would not be refused to the heart that wished it.

Under the symbols of the leopard of malice, the lion of violence and ambition, and the she-wolf of incontinence, Dante is determined to have us recognize the sins which are so easily hidden beneath justified motives and weaknesses left uncontrolled. From hopeless limbo to the frozen lake of Cocytus, Dante drags us down mercilessly through our own inner journey. He teaches us that there is violence in the heart that blasphemes and scorns the gifts of Nature, and that there is no pity for those "who waste the good and substance of their lives and weep in that sweet time when they should be gay." All are descriptions of distortions of beings whose weight of guilt sink the ones who have forgotten their Creator into the pain of their own misdeeds.

Dante's strength comes from his great faith in an afterlife immersed in the glow of holiness. This very assurance of what lies at the essence of all matter and of every event makes Dante a man of little patience and no tolerance for corruption. To Nimrod, the symbolic expression of elemental forces untranscended by the light of Divine Love, the character of Virgil cries out: "Babbling fool, stick to your horn and vent yourself with it when rage or passion stir your stupid soul." In the vast architecture of his majestic allegory, Dante is careful to express straightforward truths which each attentive soul may clearly recognize.

In order to awaken his readers to the true horror of spiritual darkness, Dante plunges us into such nauseating, obscene visions of bestial depravity that, as sickened observers, we must retreat into the protective spaces of our own faith. The hope of a life in the spirit beyond death, so infinitely removed from the darkness of the grave and its shades of hell, becomes more vital than ever before. One may justifiably wonder how such monstrosities could have oozed out of this noble Italian's soul without damaging his own hope for purification.

Such reasoning leads one to consider the epoch in which Dante lived and the surrounding images of those grisly times. There was no possibility of concealing oneself from the constant reminders of one's own mortality. Temporal horror was forever present and often served as fuel for the spiritual fire of the men and women whose lives were driven by experiences of transforming truth. The reality of a higher world and its powers over the transient madness of humankind were so obvious to them that the wicked themselves could not believe they were living in a godless universe. From the mouth of the tortured we hear:

Inflexible Justice that has forked and spread my soul like hay, to search it the more closely, finds in the country where my guilt was bred this increase in my grief. (c.30, 70-73)

Even the damned know the necessity of their horrific condemnation, for as Virgil voices:

"Who is more arrogant within his soul, who is more impious than one who dares to sorrow at God's judgment?"

Dante weeps and faints and cowers in terror, as anyone who follows his journey closely will do, before the repulsive depiction of the eternal atrocities inflicted upon Mahomet, or glancing at the frozen eyes of the worst of sinners lost in the deepest caverns of Hell, who, in the black desolation, gnaw forever on the skulls of their enemies.

Virgil himself declares that "the wish to hear such baseness is degrading." But Dante knows that he must give expression to his passionate consciousness of human depravity and its spiritual consequences. There is little doubt from these penetrating and troubling verses that the author must have shivered at his own fancy as he endured the voyage through symbolic agonies of remorseful conscience and just punishment, for he does not attempt to depict himself as innocent.

The awesome power of The Divine Comedy is found in the exceedingly rare fact that its begetter undergoes his own confrontation with the multiform human spirit of which he is a particle. Dante witnesses to countless centuries of unborn generations that he felt a shame so intense that "I grow pale yet at the memory."

As one trapped in a nightmare that has caught his sleeping mind, wishes within the dream that it were all a dream, as if it were not – such I became . . .(c.30, 136-139)

The utterly humbling experience of inner shame allows him to forgive himself under the guise of his guide and master, Virgil. And it is right that he do so, for that depth of shame is the hope of the Christian, since it is upon its shores that the Divine Presence may be felt approaching.

Despite the barbaric elements of Medieval culture, the purpose of life seemed clearer and more immediate to certain Christians of that period than it does to many who profess belief in this age. Self-study and great effort applied to one's awakening beyond the limits of empirical existence led to a possible experience of spiritual reality of which The Divine Comedy is one of the giant witnesses of all time. Just as nature is a projection of the sun's creative powers, so are Dante's images reflections of psychological conditions.

We inhabitants of the late twentieth century seem utterly sterilized from the awareness of the "numinous" dimension of Christianity and of our responsibility to that Whole of which we feel ourselves so strangely independent. We have become sophisticated to such a degree through the distortions of our culture, which glorifies the human being as somehow above the forces which create and destroy it, that we seem to have a much greater difficulty in coming within hearing distance of ourselves as we truly are. Sin and rebirth, or as Dante called it, "trans-human change," no longer seem to have the critical importance they represented to those distant times. In fact, those words have virtually lost all meaning whatsoever in today's bland and artificial forms of religion.

Modern psychology has invented positive attributes to anger, vanity, lust and ambition. Our churches wallow in the ideas of the day, without compass or leadership. We have used our reason to "disprove" God by reducing the Eternal Spirit to a concept. We build our castles on the sands of intellectual arrogance, scientific achievement, and naive political principles. Today, we do not concern ourselves with primitive fears of a "Hell" teeming with monsters and torments.

Lost in the meaninglessness of our soothing distractions, we can claim the progress of having created an environment in which all values are relative, holiness is superstition, and the Universe is ours to plunder and rape. But death will not be conquered, and we will each be stripped bare of our fabricated identities and material crutches when our time is up. We may then find ourselves haunted by the terrors of the dark unknown from which we come, as it demands the fruits of our earthly lives. There will be no more cheap religiosity or intellectual manipulation to muffle our consciences. Though we may not be sent across the Marshes of Styx into the bowels of the earth, we will each be alone in the dark and terrifying wood of our errors and ignorance. What we will know then only a soul of Dante's stature can put to paper.

Thus you may understand that love alone is the true seed of every merit in you, and of all acts for which you must atone. (c.17, 103-105)

6

Seeking the Center
Solitude as Spiritual Awakening

In a world of noise and chaos, there is hardly anything more important to the health of the human soul than to find solitude and stillness. In the cleansing from distraction, we can realign ourselves with a natural rhythm which has been nearly lost to our twenty-first century lifestyle. It is this peace and centering that we yearn for in vacation and escape, but it is so vital to our wellbeing that we need a taste of it every day, not merely on special occasions. Some of us are so alienated from the depths of our being that we fear silence and aloneness, when in fact it is the road home to our True Self, beyond noise, beyond chaos, beyond time. These moments alone with ourselves are the foundation of an authentic spiritual life. In solitude, we find our center, and from that place, we come into deeper contact with all people.

We are all familiar with the eye of the hurricane. This is a good image for living out our spirituality in daily life. As the events swirl around us, as our emotions – and other people's – get stirred up, we need to keep one foot in that calm place. Otherwise, we are thrown out of our center and hurled into the storm. Then, as Dorothy said so well, "we're not in Kansas anymore." Anger boils, fear digs into us, imagination catches fire, depression weighs down on us, and impatience grits our teeth as we react to everything from the length of the grocery store line to the duration of the red light. For some folks, this is a recurring treadmill that seems to have no way out. But there is a way out! We are not meant to exist in this manner. When Paul says: "Rejoice in the Lord always" he isn't being a Pollyanna. When Jesus tells us "do not worry about your life," he isn't offering us a good idea but is calling us to walk on the Way, to sell all we have (our fears, requirements, habits, attitudes) and seek first the kingdom. As the Psalmist stated: "Be still and know that I Am God."

The legacy of spiritual teachings across the centuries offer us many ways in which to incorporate into our daily lives this crucial aspect of our spiritual journey. Whether we call such methods "practicing the presence of God," "centering prayer," "recollection," "mindfulness," the ancient "hesychia" (inner tranquility) or any number of names coming down to us through different traditions, the fundamentals remain the same. The aim is to establish a place of quiet within us, an inner sanctuary, where contact with the Spirit can occur and be maintained, regardless of external circumstances.

The spiritual discipline required to create such an oasis where we can remain sensitive to the "still, small voice" is both subtle and demanding. It begins as a matter of attention. Understanding that God is always present and it is we who are absent, we must disengage our attention from the things that pull us every which way so that some portion of our awareness can be retained inwardly for contact with the Spirit. Otherwise, we are "leaking cisterns" as Jeremiah called us, forever wasting our emotional energy and attention on passing things, always making "mountains out of mole hills." The popular saying "don't sweat the small stuff" is rooted in the deep wisdom of the saints who have gone before us. It's the small stuff that will steal our peace and keep us disconnected from the Presence of God.

Isn't it amazing that a small cloud can block out the sun? Self-control (one of the fruits of the Spirit) enables us to manage our use of attention during the day so we can chase the cloud away and let God be part of our reality.

Clearly, the time to create that quiet place within, the secret room where Christ tells us to go pray, is not in the midst of a crisis. It is in the ordinary pattern of our life that we need to establish such a foundation. The ancient teachers suggest that we regularly take ten minutes in the morning and ten at night, and stick to that discipline religiously. They claim that the very repetition of that small effort has a long-term impact on our psychology. Here is a simple approach to entering your center:

- Quiet the mind: Anyone who has attempted this knows that it is no easy task. We seldom reach a stage where there is absolute silence. Seek the deeper silence behind the noise of our thoughts.
- Slow your breathing: Breathe slowly and deeply. You can actually lower your blood pressure and reduce your heartbeat.
- Relax your body: Sitting with your backbone straight but not rigid allows the energy to flow with less obstruction.
- Bring your hands together: One hand placed over the other, palms up, allows the energy to circulate in the same way as connecting a circuit.
- Sit in silence: Just ten to twenty minutes a day will recharge your batteries more powerfully than several hours of sleep. It won't be long before you will want to increase that private time because it is not just refreshing, but life-giving.

The goal is to carry into all circumstances a quality of receptivity that keeps us in touch with the Spirit and therefore available to its promptings. This is how we become people of peace as well as instruments of divine blessing to others. The true purpose of this kind of spiritual discipline is revealed by the Quaker author Thomas Kelly, and bears repetition:

For though we begin the practice of secret prayer with a strong sense that we are the initiators and that by our wills we are establishing our habits, maturing experience brings awareness of being met, and tutored, purged and disciplined, simplified and made pliant in God's holy will by a power waiting within us. For God works in our souls, in their deepest depths, taking increasing control as we are progressively willing to be prepared for God's wonder.

So put time aside to sit quietly and free yourself from the hordes of thoughts crisscrossing the highways of your mind. As you will find out quickly, we can't erase those swarming mosquitoes, but we can watch them go by as boats going down a river (to quote Thomas Keating, author of "Centering Prayer"). The trick is to not get in the boat! In this way, we establish a certain inner freedom from our feelings and thoughts and start the journey of mastering ourselves, of setting our house in order. As this new center of peace and stability within us is strengthened, we gradually find that it remains with us throughout the day, not merely at times of meditation and prayer. This begins the process of truly becoming temples of the spirit.

7

Facing Our Obsessive Patterns:
The Roots of the "Seven Deadly Sins"

The behavior known as gluttony has been called in western civilization not merely a "sin" but one of the "seven deadly sins." In order to understand why it has been classified in this manner and what this behavior really is, it is necessary to learn the origins of the classification itself. Most of us who are products of the western world have no idea that these "seven deadly sins" come down to us as a derivative of another more ancient and more profound wisdom which offers us new insight into our psychology.

We have assumed that "sins," and "gluttony" in particular, carry a heavy moral weight of guilt and shame because of the way generations before us perceived it. We have here a great example of how important it is to examine our presuppositions, as they so often lead us into those unconscious assumptions which prejudice and distort our understanding.

This idea of the "seven deadly sins" is not original to the Catholic Church and is a reduction and distortion of the spiritual teaching that came before it and that has largely been lost to us. In order to recover something of the original meaning, we must return to the fourth century and the middle-eastern lands where these teachings germinated. It was the Greek monastic theologian Evagrius of Pontus who first drew up a list of eight human "passions:" *Gluttony, lust, avarice, sadness, anger, acedia (sloth), vainglory, and pride.* For Evagrius, these passions represent an increasing fixation with the self, with pride as the most egregious of them. These passions are brought into play by thoughts or images which Evagrius does not name "sins" or "vices," but rather *logismoi*, meaning distracting or afflictive thoughts. These thoughts might be identified in our day as deeply ingrained obsessive patterns that are reinforced by habit.

These obsessive thoughts undermine the spiritual life and require recognition and resistance. They are not seen as a moral failing calling for repentance. Evagrius held that spiritual progress depends on close observation of thoughts as they arise in the mind. Thoughts are symptoms, not sins. They buzz around in the mind looking for cracks in the heart – points of weakness and vulnerability. Their Greek name, *pathi* (pathology), suggests that a person is brought by them to a state of passivity and slavery. In fact, they overcome the will, so that the person victimized by his or her passions no longer has access to their free will.

Ancient writers give us a surprisingly contemporary psychotherapy of the human soul. Nilus the Ascetic writes that the stomach, by gluttony, becomes a sea impossible to fill – a good description of any passion. The objects which the passions look for cannot satisfy them because objects are finite and as such do not correspond to the unlimited thirst of the passions.

This teaching was taken over by a disciple of Evagrius, John Cassian, a monk who came to find him from the West and then returned to Gaul where he shared this spiritual wisdom and changed its emphasis. He turned the eight thoughts into eight vices, and made us responsible for holding them. Sin became a moral issue. Evagrius believed that people are only partly responsible for these *logismoi* which are external to us and therefore outside of the human will. Cassian suggested that they seek out the sin hidden in our hearts. This change of perspective led to Augustine's position that sin is basic to our human nature. Augustine became the most influential teacher in the western world for a thousand years. Cassian never acknowledged his source – Evagrius and the spiritual wisdom of the east – which is why his teaching has been lost for centuries, preserved only in eastern orthodox materials.

In the late sixth century, Pope Gregory the Great reduced the list to seven items, folding vainglory into pride, acedia into sadness, and adding envy. His ranking of the sins' seriousness was based on the degree from which they offended against love. It was, from most serious to least: pride, envy, anger, sadness, avarice, gluttony, and lust.

Gaining freedom from these likes and dislikes, according to the ancient wisdom teachings, means taming the passions. In doing so, we gain the freedom to love others by being less focused on our own desires. This does not mean that we need to deprive ourselves of good food or entertainment, but rather that we should enjoy what is necessary for our well-being, while foregoing the indulgences that arise out of our obsessive impulses.

Passions like gluttony cannot be ignored. We must recognize them and discipline them to come under the control of our mind. This discipline leads us into a lifestyle that does not undermine our health or freedom. Uncontrolled passions are like a team of wild horses pulling our wagon. We imagine that we are the driver, but the horses take us where they wish to go. The challenge is to harness our pathological tendencies so they will be obedient to the driver who is our higher potential.

The greatest error regarding gluttony is to think it pertains only to food. There are persons who cannot get enough of toys, television, entertainment, sex, or company. It is about an excess of anything. If we understand the context out of which gluttony is considered as an obsessive, pathological disorder, not merely in relation to food, but as a relationship to all things – including other people and the planet itself – then we can clearly see the impact and the dangers of this behavior. Such a holistic view of this condition enables us to find the discipline to observe and confront this uncontrolled pathology which is so destructive to the world and to ourselves. Seeing the deeper implications of gluttony as a desperate attempt to satisfy a hunger for the infinite through the consuming of the finite, we are able to refocus our yearnings in order to achieve a healthy balance and right relationship with life itself.

8

Lost Teachings of Ancient Christianity

Some of the most powerful and applicable spiritual teachings of Christianity remain unknown to the general population, even after two millennia. These teachings were preserved in monasteries and were often instructions to monks on inner warfare, internal self-awareness, on ascetical efforts, and efforts of spiritual discipline for their development and awakening to spiritual reality.

These teachings were never meant to be only for the few, specially called out people, or for people with a particular vocation. These teachings are for all people, and this science of spiritual development is one that is available to humanity, not merely to those who have special access to this material. The split between the East and the West in 1054, that is, between the Orthodox and Catholic churches, in many ways cut those of us in the West off from these profound wisdom treasures which are still as valid today as they were in the fourth, sixth and tenth centuries.

Let's take a look at one of these marvelous gifts to humanity that has come down, so hidden, though it was not meant to be. This one in particular is known as the *Watch of the Heart.* The Desert Fathers of Christianity used this approach as a central method to help people unify themselves around the consciousness of the Divine. The Watch of The Heart translates as self-observation, that is, observation of what is actually taking place within one's psychological and emotional life. Instead of taking for granted every thought and emotion that comes to us, calling it "I," and allowing it to take over in the present moment and cause all sorts of random havoc, we become more objectively aware of this activity within our minds and emotions through a process of inner separation. For instance, if thoughts enter that have negative and violent qualities, we consciously resist them rather than take them as a manifestation of our identity.

There is a graphic and rather crude expression of this methodology to be found in ancient writings which is as follows: When we see the snake coming in through the hole under the door – when the thought is about to enter your heart, take you over and cause you to act out – you must cut off the head of the snake. This forceful teaching makes it very clear that if we allow any emotion or thought to come in unguarded and enter our minds and hearts, the result is that we ascent to it, we agree with it, accept it, receive it – only to become captives of it. So, when the suggestion which initially appears to us is assented to, we become captive to it and we act out its wrongful expression. The Desert Fathers perceived that what happens is a universal phenomena: something comes into our mind, we mull it over, we let it enter into our heart, we bond with it, and then we *become* the thought or emotion.

Most of you know that we often hear a piece of music in our heads out of nowhere, and we cannot even trace where it came from – it is just stuck there. The same is true with many thoughts and emotions. Sometimes we pick them up from the environment. Think of how you feel after watching a violent horror movie. Those negative elements of fear, violence, tension or anguish fill us, and we need to be cleansed of them. So this teaching is very much a contemporary recognition of the human condition. Jesus said it loud and clear: we must cleanse the inside of the cup, meaning our inner life, our psychological life, our spiritual life. We cannot go around with heavy, negative thoughts and think that we are going to progress anywhere in the spiritual life, or please God in any way.

We certainly cannot call ourselves 'religious people' when we live in these lower states of consciousness, acting out in any old way from the darkest part of our nature. This psychological work from the Christian perspective is spiritual warfare, that is, the battle to lift ourselves out of anything that drags us down. In many ways, the world around us, our culture for example, seems to actively and aggressively seek to drag us into the lowest centers of our being. It is up to each of us to use our free will not to go that way, but to go another way, to take the Royal Road, as it has been called, and go the way of love instead of the way of judgment, which only leads to violence. We are not speaking merely of morality; we are talking about the purification of the heart. Purification is a key spiritual concept that we find down through the ages, and it begins with the simple practice of inner attention, of developing some kind of self-awareness and self-control that allows us to not be victimized continuously by whatever is going on around us.

Wouldn't it be wonderful if you could control yourself in such a way that throughout the day you remained consistent in your state of mind no matter what circumstances you find yourself in? For example, something as simple as having to wait in line at a grocery store can cause one to become impatient, stimulating the adrenal glands and all that which generates a state of mind far removed from Spirit. This is a daily work effort, and the great genius of the early teachers of Christianity was that they combined this moment-to-moment inner attention with prayer. Attention and prayer become one, so that in every moment we are conscious of the presence of God. We are in tune and in touch, invoking and enabling Spirit to work in our lives. This is, as Jesus said, a pearl of great price and truly a legacy for all people who seek that higher life which gives meaning and purpose to all that we are and all that we do, and which enables us to consciously bring the invisible into the visible realm of reality, to become part of God's mission of loving the world as our only true purpose.

May you be self-aware and attentive in discerning and freeing yourself from anything that would hold you captive and pull you down into the darkness of any negative thought or emotion. There is help. You can find it if you honestly and with right motivation seek to live out this discipline. Through the practice of uncritical self-observation, this watching of the heart, you will find your way to The Way, to the Royal Road, to the Way of Christ, the way of self-surrender, the way of consciousness of God, and become aware of the presence of God in every moment. May you find this great gift to humanity, this revelation of truth and wisdom.

9

The Individual and the Community

Common ground is central to the development of community. This does not mean that people are required to be alike. The concept of "unity in diversity" is actually a critical dynamic for authentic community. Yet while we honor the individuality and differences of each person, there must be some common bond that enables us to transcend variations in personalities, education, and culture. Because we are bound together by that common ground, we are enabled to accept and understand each other.

In one community, where the intent was to reach a place of spiritual maturity, the leader insured that there was always someone in the group whose personality was especially difficult to tolerate. In this way, people who had joined together to "work on themselves" were forced to transcend their personal preferences to such an extent that they could accept this individual and thereby learn to be in community with all varieties of persons. The teacher in this community called this method "*learning to bear the unpleasant manifestations of others.*" We all know how difficult this is to do in daily life, which is why the philosopher Jean-Paul Sartre made the famous statement: "Hell is other people." For those who seek spiritual maturity, the aim is to do our best not to be that hell for those around us and to endure with compassion and understanding the projections, dysfunction, and baggage of others. Living in community with these harsh realities requires the powerful motivation of holding something sacred in common. Otherwise, the effort and sacrifice are overwhelming.

In the religious context, this common ground comes from a shared experience and knowledge that have become such a priority for every person that it is now the axis of their lives. That individual valuation is the cornerstone for true community. This is frequently forgotten and, in some circles, it is believed that community is the opposite of individuality and therefore the individual is to give himself or herself up to that amorphous thing named "community." This is a dangerous illusion that has often led to the worst kinds of tyranny. In such cases, community can be a destroyer of people, forcing individuals into a conformity that is dehumanizing. Then the very essence of community is betrayed and people are left with some form of spiritual imprisonment. Any community that requires people to check their individuality in at the door is either a cult or a dictatorship. The community is not meant to absorb the individual, but rather to enhance his or her potential.

One of the most dramatic factors affecting the disintegration of community is the fatal element of suspicion. When trust breaks down and negative attitudes become pervasive, the community is on its last legs. Sometimes this poison of suspicion arises in individuals without any external cause. Certain people are suspicious of everything, either out of fear or need for control, which is really the same issue. They pollute the atmosphere to such an extent that it becomes unsustainable. Many communities have been destroyed by just a few such people. The old saying "one rotten apple spoils the barrel" is tragically accurate. A thriving community cannot exist with that kind of shadow. In many groups, the lack of structure or fear of conflict make it impossible to confront this death-dealing attitude. Lacking the courage to face destructive individuals for the sake of the community's future, generally insures its doom.

It is often assumed that those in positions of authority are truly loyal to the ideals of the group. But if the people in charge are not abiding by any standards of conduct that reflect the community's identity, then the very existence of that community is corrupted. What we have then is a group of people fighting it out for power and control rather than a place of nurturing, relationship, and growth. It is in such communities that we encounter the toxic behavior that is so rampant among congregations and where the possibility of spiritual development has long been abandoned.

The teachings of the Apostle Paul, who initiated Christian communities beyond Jerusalem and across the known world, often stand as an ironic contrast to the reality we witness in this day and age: *"I therefore, the prisoner in the Lord, beg you to lead a life worthy of the calling to which you have been called, with all humility and gentleness, with patience, bearing with one another in love, making every effort to maintain the unity of the Spirit in the bond of peace." - Ephesians 4: 1-3*

People seeking that kind of common ground cannot find a home in many churches because the churches are no longer what they claim to be. Once again, we are faced with the necessity of recreating authentic community in each generation. Such a state of affairs places responsibility on everyone to co-create and invest in the building of such communities. This is both a challenge and a marvelous opportunity, calling on every person to help build that which did not exist before. The fact that it is temporary and may disappear in our lifetime simply means that something new will be initiated in the future. This life cycle of communities parallels the cycle of organic life and insures the vitality and creativity that is the very nature of everything that lives.

So the next time you go into a community that has long lost sight of its purpose for being, rather than give up on the hope of finding the kind of environment you need, work to generate that group in which you can express your own passion and commitment. Then true community will manifest once again.

10

Care for the World

Getting Beyond Partial Stewardship

In the Judeo-Christian tradition, the concept of stewardship has most often been identified with giving or "tithing" as it has been called over the centuries. The ten percent concept originates from the Babylonian civilization and its "esretu" requirement which was a one tenth tax. The tithe first appears in the Old Testament encounter between Abraham and Mechilzedek, the mysterious High Priest at the dawn of History. The tithe then became Mosaic Law and served, in part, to support the Levite priests and their work in the Temple.

This foundational idea of stewardship arises out of the primeval offering which held that, from the work of our hands, the first fruits are given to that which is most holy and sacred. As with so many spiritual teachings, this concept has been reduced to an obligation rather than a spontaneous delight. It has been taken literally so that the religious ritual of an ancient agrarian culture is now applied to people of the twenty-first century regardless of the changes that have taken place over the millennia. It has also been twisted into some kind of magical tit-for-tat, whereby the giver's motivation is stimulated through the notion that giving a certain amount generates a return. In this context, stewardship is no longer the expression of our spirit manifesting its devotion to that which is most significant in life.

One thing is certain: the spirit of stewardship is not defined by a number. Reducing it to a legalistic requirement kills the very nature of that urge to care for the world. Many of us have grown up in an environment where people are pressured to give a certain percentage in order to fulfill a religious law dating back five thousand years. To this day, that mentality continues, making some feel guilty, placing others in financial jeopardy, and generating tension in communities that are supposed to be founded on good will.

This mindset is so ingrained that some people will give their ten percent regardless of what it is used for as long as they can feel good about bringing the right amount of tribute dictated by a perceived religious requirement. They condemn everyone else who does not do so and consider themselves superior for having fulfilled their obligation. This is the kind of human foolishness that turns a beautiful spiritual impulse into its opposite.

Some individuals become so fanatic in clutching to this version of stewardship that it becomes virtually suicidal. That ten percent must be extracted whether other bills can be paid or not. Under these circumstances, stewardship turns into something irrational and irresponsible. There are churches everywhere around us that are dying, in part, because they would rather serve the literal interpretation of tithing rather than regenerate their own community in order to give more in the future. Holistic stewardship includes care for the world, care for your loved ones and care for yourself.

The notion from the earliest civilizations that we must "appease the gods" through the giving of that which is precious to us must evolve into a conscious, purposeful commitment to the ultimate things of life. We then become contributors to the betterment of the world. Some have called it becoming co-creators because we incarnate something of that Spirit to which we have given ourselves. Stewardship then permeates everything we do, from the smallest act of random kindness to the greatest philanthropic gestures, and finally to a self-sacrifice in which our very existence becomes a gift. This understanding of stewardship is a far cry from the familiar ten percent concept which has for so long been the common understanding of these teachings. In this light, ten percent becomes an insult to that which is truly significant in life, some kind of petty obligation that has little to do with where our true interests lie.

The words of the Christ are clear on this matter: *"Woe to you, scribes and Pharisees, hypocrites! For you tithe mint, dill, and cummin, and have neglected the weightier matters of the law: justice and mercy and faith. It is these you ought to have practiced without neglecting the others." (Matthew 23:23)* How often have we donated money or efforts to a good cause for the primary purpose of feeling good about ourselves, of enjoying the sensation of self-righteousness. We are then able to justify all sorts of terrible behavior because we consider ourselves justified by our self-interested generosity. This is the image of hypocrisy which keeps so many seekers away from the institutional church. It is evident to all except the individual fooled by his or her own justification, that we cannot hide our lack of goodness behind one superficial act. Yet, this mindset is standard procedure and often the entire reasoning behind the concept of stewardship. "If I give this much, I don't have to do anything else."

An authentic spirit of stewardship requires each of us to devote all aspects of our lives to the care of others and of creation. Partial commitment turns stewardship into something else that has nothing to do with care. The need for stewardship on both the global and individual scale requires a commitment of all that we are and do so that it may be effectively lived out.

11

Learning to Forgive

The Spiritual Side of Mending Relationships

Most people would agree that one of the hardest spiritual teachings is to "love your enemy." Nothing could go more against the grain of our human nature than to love those who seek to do us harm. But going against the grain is precisely the Way of spiritual awakening. It is known as a path of self-denial, or better yet – self-transcendence – because the part of us that can only hate the enemy must die. The decision to follow this teaching requires a total devotion, an absolute commitment to transcend our fundamental urges for self-interest and self-preservation.

Teachers of many traditions point out that it doesn't mean much to love those who love us. Anyone can do that. Loving those who do not love us is an entry into a new way of life that opens to the Presence of God. This choice to love the enemy has to do with the very nature of spiritual evolution. If we manage to accomplish that hard task, then we will know on an intimate level something of the reality of a new consciousness of living.

To love those who not only have no love for us, but actively dislike us is to enter a quality of consciousness that is free of concern for self and for the actions of others. To love one's enemy is not weakness, but the ultimate strength, because it requires exceptional self-control and objective compassion for others without any requirements. It also calls for an inner stability that nothing can shake. People who can love their enemies are people who know their true identity. They do not need validation from the outside because they are anchored, "rooted and grounded" in a greater power.

This is certainly advanced spiritual work, the fruit of wisdom and understanding gained in the furnace of years of efforts. It is the goal of all authentic spiritual paths because the person who loves their enemies has conquered violence in themselves. The ability to accomplish what might seem impossible to our natural self, is also the key to spiritual healing. All of those wounds from our past that keep us fearful and defensive evaporate in the light of this new way of life. In order to be able to love one's enemies, one has to live from a different perspective, no longer concerned with oneself, conscious of one's true purpose in this world, free from the ways of our culture and enabled by a greater power. We access this power through breaking the chains of our emotions that keep us anchored in self-absorption.

If you have ever tasted this new consciousness and relationship to others, you will understand why it is called the pearl of great price. To be free to love your enemies is to live in unconquerable gratitude and joy.

So the question becomes: How do we go about forgiving people who have hurt us badly? This is a crucial question for all our relationships and for our own health and peace of mind. In order to realistically approach this difficult issue, it is important to recognize that sometimes people cannot control how they behave. We certainly need to be held responsible for what we do as adults, but we all know that sometimes knee-jerk reactions take over and we are as surprised as everyone else about what we have done.

Recognizing that dynamic in human behavior makes it possible for us to begin the process of forgiveness. This issue of forgiveness is critical to our well-being as much as it is to those who need to be forgiven. Holding on to resentment or anger, however justified, is very destructive and often makes people terribly ill. I know a lady from a previous congregation whose husband cheated on her for years. Sometime after their divorce, cancer developed in her body. She kept telling me that she couldn't let go of her anger and could not bring herself to forgive. The cancer eventually spread to her face and ate her up.

We hurt ourselves more than the other person by being unwilling to forgive and we keep them in control of us, even long after they are dead. This is a central teaching of all authentic spiritual wisdom and one that we cannot afford to disregard. In the New Testament, the Greek word for "forgive" means to put down, as in taking our baggage off our back and walking away from it. Life is too short to carry heavy burdens unnecessarily.

It is true that in the process of reconciliation with another person, it is important for people to admit their errors and to say those simple but difficult words "I'm sorry." This enables the relationship to go forward. A sense of conviction over our errors and remorse for them places us in a position to be given a second chance. Imagine if none of us were given another opportunity to make things right. Because we all need it, we must be willing to give it to others, even though it can be very difficult. As we learn in life, most things that are worthwhile don't come easy. It is part of our humanity to make the extra effort to overcome painful things. We are then empowered to begin anew.

Also by Theodore J. Nottingham

Yeshua the Cosmic Mystic
Beyond Religion to Universal Truth

The Wisdom of the Fourth Way
Origins and Applications of a Perennial Teaching

Written in our Hearts
The Practice of Spiritual Transformation

The Journey of the Anointed One
Breakthrough to Spiritual Encounter

Parable Wisdom
Spiritual Awakening in the Teachings of Jesus

The Spiritual Bankruptcy of the Church
The Dark Side of Modern Religion

The Desolation Chronicles
A Visionary Novel of Humanity's Future

Hugo
The Strange Life and Visions of Victor Hugo

The Untold Story of John Wilkes Booth

The Druid's Isle
The Mystical Adventures of Saint Patrick

The Color of the Wind
Fables for All Ages

The Final Prophet
(The Messiah Chronicles, Book 1)

The Journey of the Anointed One

The Tribulation
(The Messiah Chronicles, Book 2)

The Trial of Anne Hutchinson
A Play in Two Acts

Journey from Atlantis
The Perilous Adventures of a Citizen from the Lost Continent

Madman at the Wishing Well
Four Metaphysical One Act Comedies

The Enchanted Kingdom
Stories for Children

The Baron's Daughter
The Saga of the Children's Crusade

Blood on Holy Land
A Novel on the Clash between Islam and Christianity
(A Kindle version of "The Baron's Daughter")

Missives from an Outsider
Five Metaphysical Short Stories

Translations
by Theodore & Rebecca Nottingham

The Power of the Name
The History and Practices of the Jesus Prayer
(by Alphonse & Rachel Goettmann)

The Spiritual Wisdom & Practices of Early Christianity
(by Alphonse & Rachel Goettmann)

The Beyond Within Initiation into Meditation
(Alphonse & Rachel Goettmann)

The Path of Initiation
An Introduction to the Life and Thought of Karlfried Graf Durckheim
(by Alphonse Goettmann)

Becoming Real
Essays on the Teachings of a Master
(Edited by Alphonse & Rachel Goettmann)

Also published by Theosis Books with a Foreword by Theodore J. Nottingham

Spiritual Metamorphosis
The Awakening of the Human Heart
(by Efstratios Papanagiotou)

Divinization
The Hidden Teaching within Divine Wisdom
(by Efstratios Papanagiotou)

The Inner Restoration of Christianity
(by Efstratios Papanagiotou)

The Transformation of Suffering
Charles B. Ashanin's Theology of Humanity's Evolution
(by Peter Haskins)

Also Published by Theosis Books

Practical Christianity
Practicing the spiritual Teachings of Christianity in Daily Life
(by Rebecca Nottingham)

The Fourth Way and Esoteric Christianity
An Introduction to the Teachings of G.I. Gurdjieff
(by Rebecca Nottingham)

Fourth Way Teachings
Practical Methods on Inner Transformation
(by Rebecca Nottingham)

Lightning Source UK Ltd.
Milton Keynes UK
UKOW06f1915210915

259023UK00008B/222/P

9 780983 769712